# BALM IN
# GILEAD

SAMUEL RONICKER

WESTBOW
PRESS®
A DIVISION OF THOMAS NELSON
& ZONDERVAN

Scripture taken from the New King James Version®. Copyright © 1982 by Thomas Nelson. Used by permission. All rights reserved.

WestBow Press books may be ordered through booksellers or by contacting:

WestBow Press
A Division of Thomas Nelson & Zondervan
1663 Liberty Drive
Bloomington, IN 47403
www.westbowpress.com
1 (866) 928-1240

ISBN: 978-1-9736-1498-2 (sc)
ISBN: 978-1-9736-1499-9 (hc)
ISBN: 978-1-9736-1497-5 (e)

Library of Congress Control Number: 2018900538

Print information available on the last page.

WestBow Press rev. date: 02/08/2018

Also by Sam Ronicker

*Letters to Shelley*
*Sermons From a Tiny Pulpit*
*The Greatest Sermon Ever Preached*

# Balm in Gilead
# Devotions for the Wounded Heart
# PREFACE

The prophet Jeremiah asks, "Is there no balm in Gilead? Is there no physician there?" Yes, Jeremiah there is balm in Gilead to make the wounded whole as the old hymn goes.

This devotional is balm for wounded hearts. Those wounded hearts who wonder at times, is God really there? Does God really care?

We have all been wounded in the battle of life in this broken world. This devotional is a chance to step back from the conflict for a minute and take some refreshment, put some balm on that wounded heart and know more deeply than ever that God is there and God does care.

Dr. Sam understands the wounded heart. As a missionary, counselor, pastor, educator, and businessman he has been in the thick of the battle for many, many years. His heart had taken many direct hits from family, friends, ministry partners, students, and even members of his congregation.

He is able to take a realistic look at life and at God. You will find no political correctness here, no 'Sunday School' answers, no phony Jesus but the real thing. Only reality can heal those wounds, something missing in the North American Church over the last several decades.

Grab your Bible and come on along and see. You will enjoy the straight forward talk, you will smile at the silliness that we sometimes accept as truth and tradition, and you will grow in the knowledge of the Lord as the Scriptures apply their healing balm straight to your heart.

# INTRODUCTION

*The Good News*

"Now on the first day of the week Mary Magdalene came to the tomb early, while it was still dark, and saw that the stone had been taken away from the tomb. So she ran and went to Simon Peter and the other disciple, the one whom Jesus loved, and said to them, 'They have taken the Lord out of the tomb, and we do not know where they have laid him.' So Peter went out with the other disciple, and they were going toward the tomb. Both of them were running together, but the other disciple outran Peter and reached the tomb first. And stooping to look in, he saw the linen cloths lying there, but he did not go in. Then Simon Peter came, following him, and went into the tomb. He saw the linen cloths lying there, and the face cloth, which had been on Jesus' head, not lying with the linen cloths but folded up in a place by itself. Then the other disciple, who had reached the tomb first, also went in, and he saw and believed; for as yet they did not understand the Scripture, that he must rise from the dead."
—John 20:1-9

"While they were perplexed about this, behold, two men stood by them in dazzling apparel. And as they were frightened and bowed their faces to the ground, the men said to them, 'Why do you seek the living among the dead? He is not here, but has risen.'" —Luke 24:4-6

"So they departed quickly from the tomb with fear and great joy, and ran to tell his disciples. And behold, Jesus met them and said, 'Greetings!'

And they came up and took hold of his feet and worshiped him." —
Matthew 28:8-9

"Jesus said to her, 'I am the resurrection and the life. He who believes in Me, though he may die, he shall live. And whoever lives and believes in Me shall never die. Do you believe this?'" —John 11:25-26

# DO YOU HAVE ANYTHING TO EAT?

*Luke 24:36-43*

Resurrection Sunday is the greatest single day known in the history of the world. It's The Day when Jesus rises from the dead to prove that he is God the Son and that God the Father is satisfied with Jesus' sacrifice. It is finished, he said on the cross, it's over, it's done with, I won. And just to prove that this is all true, I will rise again on Sunday morning!

Now just think for a moment just how awesome the events of the last few days of Jesus' life have been. Think about how confusing all of this has been for the disciples and family and believers.

In Luke 24 we see a couple of folks walking to Emmaus from Jerusalem and they are talking about everything that just happened and they are confused- they don't understand it all- yet.

What does it take for us to 'get it'? Think about that for a minute. Are there things in life that I believe, that I know to be true but I just don't get it? Why sure there are.

Look at Luke 24, back up to verse 33. The two folks walking to Emmaus are met by Jesus, He sits down to dinner with them, their eyes are opened to see that it's him and he disappears.

They jump up and hustle back to Jerusalem and find the eleven disciples gathered together talking about everything that happened today. If we put all of the Gospel accounts together we know that Jesus was seen on five different times on Resurrection Sunday: by Mary Magdalene alone in the garden (John 20:14), by the women as they were going to tell the disciples (Matt. 28:9), by Peter alone, by the two disciples going to Emmaus, and now in just a minute ...

Do you wonder what they are talking about? Are they trying to put it all together? Are they trying to figure out if it's real? Now really Peter, are you sure it was Jesus? Mary was thinking it was the gardener ... and you two from Emmaus, you mean you walked nearly seven miles with Jesus before you figured out it was Him?

I know one guy who didn't believe it at all: Thomas. Doubting Thomas. He was probably saying, you know after such a traumatic experience you are all suffering from PTSD, manifest as visions of what you want to happen, how you wish it to be. Here, take a pill and get a good night's sleep.

No, I tell you it really was Jesus! Now, now, you know that gardener looks a lot like Jesus with a shorter beard ...

You have to love verse 36: while they are talking about all of this, Jesus appears right in the middle of them. And look at what He says- oh, this so like Jesus, Lamb of God, humble servant still, He says, Shalom.

Now I don't know about you but if all of a sudden Jesus appeared right here in the middle of us I think I would expect Him to say something a little more profound- he is God. But what does God say when he appears after rising from the dead? Hi everyone, just your standard Jewish greeting: Shalom. That's what they say when they answer the telephone in Israel: Shalom. Maybe it's me but I was expecting something just a little more formal ...

Verse 37: They don't even say hi back, they are scared to death, terrified and frightened, thinking that they are seeing a ghost.

Now there's one that Thomas hadn't thought of earlier, it can't be Jesus or a vision caused by PTSD, it must be His ghost. Told you ghosts were real.

Verse 38-39: Jesus knows what they are thinking. Why are you troubled? Why do you doubt? Did you really think I was the gardener? I'm much better looking than he is ... Look at my hands and feet, touch me and see. Silly people, ghosts don't have flesh and bones. It really is Me.

Verse 40: and He showed them His hands and feet, the scars from the Cross. What emotions were they feeling right then? Did they remember how they had all abandoned Him? Jesus is offering forgiveness just as He does today, for us. We have all abandoned Him one way or another. Here's the chance to be forgiven.

Verse 41: As this all sinks in they think it's just too good to be true. Don't we still feel that way? You mean salvation is free? Forgiveness of sins is free? All I really have to do is accept it? Yes, it really is that simple.

Verses 42-43: This is life changing stuff, no, this is eternity changing stuff. This determines where we will spend forever ... and what does Jesus say? Hey, you got anything to eat around here?

He turned water into the best wine you ever tasted. Jesus fed 5,000 people in one sitting. If that didn't impress anybody, He did it again with 4,000. He just rose from the dead and what does ask for? You have anything to eat? I was going to have dinner in Emmaus earlier but all they had was bread ... What? Have we got anything to eat? Our eternal souls are on the line here, we are wavering in our belief, and Jesus wants to know if we've got anything to eat? That is so like Jesus, He is just, so, so real.

And that is the whole point: He is so real. This is not a ghost, this is not a PTSD induced vision, this isn't the gardener, this is Jesus. Crucified, buried, and now risen from the dead. And He wasn't just mostly dead, He was completely dead. See His hands, His feet, His side? And now He is as real as ever standing right in front of them, eating a piece of fish.

That makes all the difference in the world to us. You mean that Jesus eating a piece of fish is that important? I tell you that it is. It proves that he is risen, he is real, it's his real body. Ghosts don't have flesh and blood he said, and my guess is that ghosts don't eat broiled fish either. It really, really, really, is Jesus.

And that gives us all great hope for our own resurrection. Someday, someday this body will put off corruption, I Corinthians 15:42-43: So also *is* the resurrection of the dead. *The body* is sown in corruption, it is raised in incorruption. It is sown in dishonor, it is raised in glory. It is sown in weakness, it is raised in power.

As was Jesus raised from the dead in incorruption, glory, and power, so will we be! Think about it- we will be like Jesus. First thing I'll say, 'you got anything to eat around here?'

Back to Luke 24: 44-47 All these things must be fulfilled, everything written all those centuries ago in the Old Testament had to come true, and they did. That's why I believe that someday I'll be like Jesus; everything else the Bible says has come true. Why would God be spoofing about our resurrection?

And He opened their understanding that they might understand the Scriptures. That's what I want! Open my understanding so I might see you all the more clearly Jesus!

And one more thing, verse 47: the news is too good to keep to yourselves. Repentance and remission of sins should be preached, in his name to all nations, starting right here in Jerusalem.

Seriously, we're talking about resurrection from the dead here and eternal consequences. How in the world can we keep that to ourselves?

Resurrection Sunday is the greatest single day known in the history of the world. It's The Day when Jesus rises from the dead to prove that He is God the Son and that God the Father is satisfied with Jesus' sacrifice. It is finished, He said on the cross, it's over, it's done with, I won. It's done. All you have to do is accept it. because it is real, Jesus is real, Jesus is alive.

This day started something new for Him too- His resurrection body. Let's start the season new: with Jesus.

I Corinthians 15 again: Now if Christ is preached that He has been raised from the dead, how do some among you say that there is no resurrection of the dead? But if there is no resurrection of the dead, then Christ is not risen. And if Christ is not risen, then our preaching *is* empty and your faith *is* also empty. Yes, and we are found false witnesses of God, because we have testified of God that He raised up Christ, whom He did not raise up—if in fact the dead do not rise. For if *the* dead do not rise, then Christ is not risen. And if Christ is not risen, your faith *is* futile; you are still in your sins! Then also those who have fallen asleep in Christ have perished. If in this life only we have hope in Christ, we are of all men the most pitiable.

Well, let me tell you- we are not people most pitiable because Christ is risen from the dead. See His hands, His feet? Is it too good to be true? He'll prove it: got anything to eat around here it's nearly lunch time?

# GROWING UP

*Romans 5:1-5*

*Ephesians 4:11-16*

Do you like cold, snowy weather? Last week I was talking about how the weather can affect our mood- dark dreary days can make us grumpy, especially when we are expecting sunshine and warmer temperatures! We had snow on the ground two days this week for goodness sake.

Well, I don't know why but I get grumpy when the weather doesn't meet my expectations. That is really kind of silly isn't it?

Have you ever noticed small children? They are not bothered by the weather at all. Oh, they may be disappointed for a minute that they cannot go outside and ride their bikes, although a little snow wouldn't bother my grandchildren, Samuel and Sophie. Weather seems to never bother children.

We talk about being children, children of God, being like a child to enter the Kingdom. Maybe that's a place in life that I need to be more child-like: not letting the weather bother me.

Well, after learning to be children of God we know that eventually we do have to grow up in certain areas of life. Paul told the Ephesians that we should no longer be children, tossed to and fro and carried about with every wind of doctrine ...

We should remain God's children and child-like forever but grow up in Christ enough to be discerning in these times; to know the truth and to not be fooled.

I've been thinking about spiritual growth all this week or so. How do we grow in Christ? What is spiritual growth? How do we grow up without becoming old and grumpy? How do we maintain a child-like attitude toward the weather without being immature?

I looked up some interesting ideas about spiritual growth, glanced at a book about the 10 steps to spiritual growth etc. etc.

A common theme I found in all of these 'how to' books; the four keys to spiritual growth:

1. Read your Bible daily
2. Meet with other believers regularly
3. Get involved in a ministry group
4. Pray daily

Really? Is that right? Is that what Jesus says, what the Bible says? Read which part of my Bible daily? Meet other believers for coffee? Involved in ministry, to Hatti? Pray daily? That's not enough for me ...

Who made these rules anyway? None of them sound like what we read in Romans 5: tribulation produces perseverance; perseverance produces character; character produces hope. Hope doesn't disappoint because the love of God has been poured out in our hearts by the Holy Spirit.

Well, somebody, somewhere had to come up with these four things, and indeed they did: "Spiritual formation is an intentional Christian practice much like that of Eastern Mysticism, which claims as its goal the development of religious maturity that leads to Christian devoutness which has its roots in the ancient practices found in those of Catholic religious orders, Ascetics and others. One engages in spiritual formation through:

Ancient Christian religious activities (prayer, the study of scripture, fasting, simplicity, solitude, confession, worship, etc.)"

Now isn't that interesting? These are left over pagan practices, we just plug in Christian things to make them Christian I suppose?

We pray to God instead of the gods from Roman and Greek times, we study the Bible instead of the pagan how-to texts, we still fast and confess and worship ...

It sounds like spiritual yoga, or some other mystical eastern discipline, like Buddhism or reaching an enlightened state of Hinduism.

I think I begin to see the problem. I think I begin to see why the four steps or ten steps or however many a particular author has identified; I see now why it never worked for me. You heard right, the four steps never worked for me.

Now in case you think that I've gone crazy and left the faith: pastor said that reading the Bible, praying and tithing or fasting or whatever those steps were, don't work for his spiritual growth. Yeah, I guess I did say that ...

But look, there is nothing wrong with being in the Word, we should be in the Word not just four verse every morning or a chapter from Proverbs every morning or whatever. Peter said we should desire the pure milk of the Word. Desire, that's the key word here, desire the pure milk of the Word! I want to Know God better through the Word! It's not something I just do, like yoga.

Prayer is good, no change that to prayer is everything! Pray without ceasing Paul told the Thessalonians.

Quiet time with God is good, be still and know he tells us.

But all these things miss one key point for spiritual growth. Look at Ephesians chapter 4, verses 11-16.

Verse 11 points out special gifts that we are given, verse 12 begins to tell us why: for equipping the saints for the work. Don't stop there: for the edifying of the body of Christ. (Edifying means to instruct especially so as to encourage intellectual, moral, or spiritual improvement.)

Don't stop there, see verse 13: till we all come to unity, knowledge of the Son of God to the measure of the fullness of Christ.

Wow that all sounds really good, like spiritual growth but don't stop there, 14: no longer be children fooled ...

Verse 15: grow up in all things into Him who is the head,

Verse 16: the whole body ...

Do you see it now? Verse 16 again: according to the effective working by which every part does its share cause growth of the body.

Paul is referring to the Body of Christ, the Church, the real Church capital C of which he, Christ is the Head. And we are the different parts of this Body, capital B, the children of the Living God, born again believers.

See it really is pretty simple- the whole body has to grow together. Individuals can't grow it alone. (Cute play on words). Oh, I suppose we can but then the body looks a little silly doesn't it? If only the right arm is being exercised then I suppose we look like Popeye and the whole body, the whole church is out of balance.

Here is the key: we grow together or usually not at all. Now you know why the four keys don't work for me. I don't grow well alone, verse 16 causes growth of the body for the edifying of itself in love.

Let that sink in for a minute: growth of the body for the edifying (to instruct especially so as to encourage intellectual, moral, or spiritual improvement) of itself in love. Performing some disciplines rooted in mystical eastern practice doesn't work for me, for us. We need each other.

We grow together as a body, the Body of Christ. That's the way Jesus designed it.

Let's try it! Let's truly instruct each other especially so as to encourage intellectual, moral, or spiritual improvement. Let's have the whole body grow together.

You can read on in Ephesians 4 as Paul writes about the 'how to' of what individuals do to grow as a body, the Body.

And I want you to think about: when people visit your church, what does the Body look like? Do they see us encouraging intellectual, moral, or spiritual improvement?

Or do they see us lopsided, like Popeye? With one big strong right arm? Let's grow together; it really is the only way.

# YOU TALKIN' TO ME?

*Ephesians 2:1-10*

It's been a beautiful week here: sun shine, warmer temperatures, it's beginning to dry out, the grass is starting to grow. We put our baby chicks out in the coop where we brood chickens and we put pigs in the outdoor pen and cleaned out the barn, cleaned out the loafing shed and cleaned out the chicken coop.

The boys at school have been reading one chapter of Proverbs every day, starting the day out with some nourishment of spiritual wisdom. Sometimes they get it, sometimes they just blast through the verses but God's word never returns void.

Once in a while a spiritual nugget will get into their minds and into their hearts.

There is something interesting about the way they read Proverbs, really the way they read most of Scripture. My wife, Teresa and I like to talk about the Proverbs study we're doing in Sunday School and we noticed this- we seem to forget sometimes just who God is speaking to in the Scriptures.

We like to read a Proverb, 15:5 for example "A fool despises his father's instruction, but he who receives correction is prudent."

And we say, yeah, I know a lot of fools who don't take advice, especially my advice.

Or verse 7: "The lips of the wise disperse knowledge, but the heart of the fool does not do so." See that's just what I'm talking about!

"A wise son makes a glad father, but a foolish son is the grief of his mother," see kids, you need to listen to me! Man, I can think of a lot of kids that are foolish and have grieved their parents.

Do you see the irony? Most importantly do you see the irony for you? Do I see the irony for me?

It always tickles me when we stumble across a Bible verse "Wisdom is on the lips of him who has understanding, but a rod is for him who is devoid of understanding," (10.13) and we say something like, yeah, that sounds like our politicians doesn't it? They need to read the Proverbs.

I'm going to share a life truth with you: Proverbs was not written for our politicians. Proverbs was not written for the our boys on the farm or their parents. Here it is, ready? Proverbs was written for me, for you.

The way to really get anything out of Scripture is to think, what is God saying to me? Not what is God saying to someone else - what is He saying to me? This is written for me.

We could go over this all day in Proverbs but you get the point. Two Proverbs that prove it:

Proverbs 19.6 "Most men proclaim each his own goodness, but who can find a faithful man?"

Proverbs 19.9 "Who can say, ' I have made my heart clean, I am pure from sin?'"

Something pretty serious to think about as look to the verses we read in Ephesians, chapter 2. These are written for me, for you.

I have a friend who is on a Walk to Emmaus this weekend, Scott T. from Columbus. Scott is an interesting character, he was saved later in life, nearly fifty. He and his wife were divorced, he got saved, she got saved and they remarried. It's a really cool story.

I've never been on a Walk to Emmaus but many folks I know have and I guess there is a time during the weekend where they are presented with encouraging letters from friends and family- I've written quite a few and was asked to write Scott.

These verses came to mind while I was working on the letter. Verse 1: who were dead. Jesus didn't just come to make sick people well, He came to make dead people alive!

Verse 2: not just dead, but walking with the world, and not just the world, but with Satan. The prince of the power of the air, the spirit who works in the sons of disobedience.

Verse 3: there's more conducted in the lusts of the flesh and the mind, and there's more- children of wrath.

Wow, that describes my old buddy Scott to a 't'. He was dead, following Satan and the world system -- still see some of those bad habits in his life today, disobedient, fulfilling the desires and lusts of the flesh- no wonder his wife left him! A real child of wrath ...

I still don't get it do I? Paul didn't write this letter to the Ephesians for my old buddy, Scott. Here's something that may surprise you: Paul did not write this letter for the Ephesians. Oh, he surely did write it to the Ephesians, it says so right in verse 1.

It might be to the saints in Ephesus, but that's not who it's for; it's for me. You. Us. The saints at your church, and each one of us individually. Scott might be an interesting character and have a cool story but it's no different than my story. It's no different than your story. Only the names change ...

I was dead in trespasses, disobedient, living in the lust of the flesh and the desires of the flesh, a child of wrath, a child of Satan. It's your story too- look closely at verse 3 and see that Paul changes pronouns. He was saying you, you were dead, and now says 'we'. We all conducted once conducted ourselves ...

Paul is one of the people this letter is written for! We all. Sometimes we just forget where we came from don't we? Sometimes we forget how we were before and sometimes even after we were saved.

But that isn't the end of the story- it's good to know where we came from or we'll forget that this book is written for us, but it's more important to know where we're going.

Verse 4: my favorite words, But God. But God didn't leave us dead, following Satan and living after the lust of the flesh.

But God, rich in mercy, because of His great love, made us alive. Let that thought sink for a minute. When we were dead, He made us alive. He made us alive, nothing that we did, nothing. That's the toughest concept to accept.

Proverbs 19:6 and 9 "Most men proclaim each his own goodness, but who can find a faithful man?" "Who can say, ' I have made my heart clean, I am pure from sin?'"

Somehow we think that we chose God, we chose to accept Jesus free gift of Salvation, we did something. That leads us to think that these verses are written for politicians, for my old buddy Scott, for Paul and the Ephesians. Well land's sake the Ephesians were idol worshipers and Paul murdered Christians. I've never done any such thing as bad as that.

Verse 8-9 again. Does this make you think differently about these very familiar verses? Does it make you think differently about how you will read this book? Does it make you think differently about how you see yourself, other Christians, other people?

God chose you, me, us. We did not chose ourselves. And He gave us the Scriptures, for us.

Let's remember that as we read and study the Bible ourselves and together.

I was thinking of Luke chapter 7 where Jesus says of the woman of ill repute: who is forgiven much, loves much, who is forgiven little, loves little.

Have you been forgiven much? I have, my friend Scott has, my guess is that all have whether we admit it or not. Let's be sure it shows in our life for Jesus!

# TRUTHS ABOUT GOD

*Daniel 2:20-23*

I finished up a lecture series this week, a verse by verse study of the Book of Daniel. Most times I like these studies- the professor who gives the lectures and he has a great tone of voice and such a way of talking that you close your eyes and can see yourself there.

This one was a little different though- he spent the first couple of weeks just on the history around the book. I kept thinking, come on – let's get on with it! And eventually he did. I probably learned more history from Daniel than I did future events and that's ok too.

This got me to thinking about what uncertain times. Do you believe that we are living in uncertain times? Has our security here in the United States of America been compromised over the past several years? Are we better off today than we were fifteen to twenty years ago? Were there decades in America that really were 'the good old days'?

Consider God's servant Daniel and his three companions Hananiah, Mishael, and Azariah. You may better remember them from your Sunday School years as Shadrach, Meshach, and Abed-Nego.

From biblical and historical evidence, we can tell that Daniel and his friends were enjoying the good life as young men in Jerusalem. They were part of the upper class, destined to be the political and religious rulers of their people. They were living in what soon would become the good old days.

Open to Daniel chapter 1: "In the third year of the reign of Jehioakim king of Judah, Nebuchadnezzar king of Babylon came of Jerusalem and the Lord gave Jerusalem to him. Then the king instructed Ashpenaz, to bring some of the children of Israel and some of the king's descendants and some of the nobles, young men in whom *there was* no blemish, but good-looking, gifted in all wisdom, possessing knowledge and quick to understand, who *had* ability to serve in the king's palace." And thus ended the good old days for Daniel and his company.

Daniel has been removed from his homeland, taken to an enemy land, and begun an indoctrination designed to de-culture his Jewish roots and re-culture him into the Babylonian lifestyle and language. Today we would call their training 'brainwashing'.

Consider the king, Nebuchadnezzar: Whomever he wished, he executed; whomever he wished, kept alive; whomever he wished, he set up; and whomever he wished, he put down, says Daniel 5:19 We can say for sure that he was living in unsettled times.

But Daniel knew that he was living in times of fulfilled prophecy. Jerusalem had fallen and been laid waste by Nebuchadnezzar just as the prophets had warned. Isaiah said 'Your own sons will be taken to Babylon' and Daniel was living proof of the truth of God's Word.

These were times of great personal turmoil for Daniel. Early on his captivity his own life was at risk unless the magicians, astrologers, the sorcerers, and the Chaldeans could tell Nebuchadnezzar his ream and interpret it. And we know that God protected Daniel and gave him the wisdom to do so.

His life was in danger again when Darius the Mede ordered him thrown into the lion's den for worshiping God rather than Darius. And again God protected him. Daniels' visions and thoughts greatly troubled him as he is praying and fasting in sackcloth and ashes.

During the third year of Cyrus' reign, Daniel is in mourning for three full weeks, as this is the time of his persecution from governors and satraps who seek to accuse him. This is time of a remnant of his people returning to Jerusalem and Daniel now realizes that he will never see his beloved homeland again; he is not part of the group that returns.

These are uncertain times, unsettled times for Daniel.

But Daniel knows something that will see him through these times: he knows the God of heaven, the God of gods, the Lord of kings, the revealer of secrets. Daniel knows God, and His Word. Daniel knows truth.

Turn to Daniel, chapter two, beginning with verse 20 we read Daniel's blessing of the God of Heaven. Daniel has received an answer to his prayer; he has received an answer to Nebuchadnezzar's dream and he thanks the Lord with seven blessings of truth. And hold your finger or book mark in the book of Job- Do you think Daniel had a copy of the Scriptures? We know he had Jeremiah, but some of the prophets are not written yet. It sure looks like he had a copy of the book of Job.

Daniel 2:20: "Daniel answered and said, Blessed be the name of God forever and ever ..." Daniel knows the Lord and knows His Word from the Book of Job 1:21, "The Lord gave and the Lord has taken away; blessed be the name of the Lord." Yet in all his trial and turmoil, 'Job did not sin.' Neither did Daniel.

Daniel 2:20: "...For wisdom and might are His," prays Daniel as did Job so many years before him. Job 12:13, "With Him are wisdom and strength, he has counsel and understanding." This is the second truth of our God.

Daniel 2:21: "And He changes the times and the seasons;" God asks Job, "Can you bring out Mazzaroth in its season? Can you guide the Great Bear with its cubs?" Job 38:32 Our God is in control, Oh greatly beloved, fear not! He made the seasons and controls the seasons.

Daniel 2:21: "He removes kings and raises up kings;" proclaims Daniel in his prayer as a fourth truth about our God. "He makes nations great, and destroys them; he enlarges nations, and guides them," spoke God's servant Job. (Job 12:23)

"Behold, the nations are as a drop in a bucket, And are counted as the small dust on the scales;" Wrote the prophet Isaiah hundreds of years later in Isaiah 40:15

Daniel 2:21: "He gives wisdom to the wise and knowledge to those who have understanding." Our Lord has wisdom, is wisdom, and freely provides wisdom to those who seek Him. Proverbs 2:6 For the Lord gives wisdom; from His mouth come knowledge and understanding." Our Lord is generous with His wisdom.

Daniel 2:22: "He reveals deep and secret things; He knows what is in the darkness ..." God has revealed Nebuchadnezzar's dream to Daniel to preserve his life. Daniel experienced this truth in a personal way.

Job knew this truth about God: "He uncovers deep things out of darkness, and brings the shadow of death to light." (Job 12:22) What could be a darker secret than the shadow of death?

Yet we need not fear, Daniel 2:22 "...and light dwells with Him." "Where is the way to the dwelling of light?" our Lord asked Job. (Job 38:19)

When we later see God in the person of Jesus Christ we will know that light does not just dwell with him, it is him. He is the very light of the world, no darkness can withstand the living God.

His name is blessed, wisdom and might are his, he controls the times and the seasons, he raises and removes the kingdoms of the earth, he gives wisdom, knowledge, and understanding to those who seek, he reveals mysteries and knows what is in the darkness, and light dwells in him. This is your God oh greatly beloved, and we understand why Daniel is told to fear not!

Who is greater than God? Who is to be trusted more than God?

Daniel's response is appropriate, Daniel 2:23: "I thank You and praise You, O God of my fathers; You have given me wisdom and might, and now have made known to me what we asked of You ..." Which brings us to an understanding of one more truth: God keeps his Word.

God does as he says, as he promises. He cannot lie, he is not a man, he is God. He is our God.

Daniel is called God's greatly beloved. And so are we. The truths that belonged to Daniel as an exile in Babylon all those years ago, belong to us, today. Even in these uncertain times. Even in these unsettled times.

What a privilege it is to know and bless the Lord.

Look to the very last chapter, 12. These are uncertain times, our future is unknown to all but our Heavenly Father. But we see more clearly every day as the end times unfold before us. Daniel was told, "Go your way, for the words are closed up and sealed till the time of the end." Daniel 12:9 We are the privileged generation to open the seal of our understanding and to trust the Lord our God to be true to his Word. Like Daniel, we are living in a time of fulfilled prophecy; the last fulfilled prophecies.

Blessed is he who waits! And patient we must be. But we can be comforted with the very words that comforted Daniel when he was told, "Go your way, till the end; for you shall rest, and will arise to your inheritance as the end of days." (Daniel 12:13)

Rest oh greatly beloved and fear not. For you will rise to your inheritance at the end of days; nearer than we know.

Did you see Anne Graham in the news recently? She said how confident she was that Rapture would happen in her lifetime and of course the media was all over that. Well, some of the media.

Will it happen in our lifetimes? Maybe, maybe not. That part of the story is sealed up, not for us to know. Be patient God says more than once in Scripture, wait on the Lord we are told.

One thing is for sure, whether we enter into rest like Daniel or are raptured first- we surely will rise to our inheritance at the end of days. It says so right here.

# VARIOUS EXHORTATIONS

I *Thessalonians 5:12-28*

Once again I have come across a passage of Scripture that I have read many, many times over the years and now I see something new. One of the verses, I Thessalonians 5:14, we have used for years at school. Every time I speak to churches or clubs or whatever about Operation Rebirth I always quote that verse as a job description of what we do.

Now we exhort you, brethren, warn those who are unruly, comfort the fainthearted, uphold the weak, be patient with all. I Thessalonians 5:14

Doesn't that sound like a great job description? Warn the unruly: hey, don't do that! Comfort the fainthearted, sometimes people just needs a hug. Uphold the weak, we encourage guys that yeah, you can do it, you can algebra, you can make a perfect bead with that welder. Be patient with all. I think he means all, everyone.

In our staff meeting this week we were looking at some of these verses and jokingly said, that's the toughest part of our job description: be patient with all! I want God to fix it now, please. I want people to hear that their sins are forgiven when they know Jesus Christ as Savior, and right away understand and be born again.

I want it to happen right now. But things don't work that way do they? God is much more patient than I am. He will wait and wait and wait before bringing judgement upon sin. I want to get it over with.

Last week some friends were talking about getting baptized- not in a church, they want something a little more exotic I guess, like Kiser Lake or the Mad River. There is no place deep enough in Mosquito Creek is there? Knowing how impatient I am you know what I'm thinking: get in the car, let's go, what are you waiting for? I am a Baptist for goodness sakes, let's get you in the water as soon as possible. Be patient with all. I think that God is talking to me in that verse. Well, I guess I have to wait until they are ready ...

Funny thing, I pulled out Dr. Robert Gromacki's *New Testament Survey* to see what he had to say about these verses, and he calls them a job description, for the church!

The heading in the New Kings James version of the Bible for these verses says, 'various exhortations.' The word that Paul uses for exhort could mean to call to one's side, call for, summon 2) to address, speak to, (call to, call upon), which may be done in the way of exhortation, entreaty, comfort, instruction, etc. I think that Paul does not 'exhort' the church to do anything that he does not do himself.

Come along side me church and do these things that I about to give you in your job description says Paul:

Verse 12- 13 And we urge you, brethren, to recognize those who labor among you, and are over you in the Lord and admonish you, and to esteem them very highly in love for their work's sake. Be at peace among yourselves.

Urge is the word Paul uses here, a little softer than exhort, but we clearly understand- recognize those who labor among you and are over you in the Lord. Who is he talking about? Church leaders. Recognize your church leaders, in the Lord. Where does any leadership come from? In the Lord, from God. And esteem them highly in love. And I'll bet you know what word Paul uses for love: agape, the strongest word he could find. Total, unconditional love.

Be at peace among yourselves. Ever feel like the church is not at peace? It starts right here- something must be missing.

Paul switches from urging to exhorting in the next two verses, imperative verbs, meaning do this!

And verse 14 again: Now we exhort you, brethren, warn those who are unruly, comfort the fainthearted, uphold the weak, be patient with all. I don't think any study is needed, just action. Warn, comfort, uphold, be patient. Do this says Paul, it's the job description of the church.

One point I want to make before we go on: There will be in all societies some who walk disorderly and it is not only the duty of preachers, but of all Christians, to warn and reproach them. Such should be scolded for their sin, warned of their danger, and told plainly of the injury they do their own souls, and the hurt they may do to others. Discipline is not just my job, it's your job, it's our job.

Verse 15: See that no one renders evil for evil to anyone, but always pursue what is good both for yourselves and for all. Evil for evil- we say it in today's English as two wrongs do not make a right.

Notice the change in sentence structure from Paul: verse 12, we urge, verse 14, we exhort, verse 15 see that it does not happen. This is a command and he continues with commands through verse 22. I'm not asking politely, Paul would say, I am telling you to do this.

And the last half of 15: pursue what is good both for yourselves and for all. Good, profitable, worthwhile, I think that word seems easy enough but go on: for yourselves. Ooh, that sounds so shellfish, pursue what is good for ourselves? For me? I thought others always come first?

It really is this simple: how do you know if something is good for all? It will be good for you, for yourselves. Think of it this way: if I pursue evil, lying cheatin' stealin' whatever it is, will it be good for me? Of course not! So it won't be good for all either!

Purse what is good, for us and for all.

Verse 16-18: Rejoice always, pray without ceasing, in everything give thanks; for this is the will of God in Christ Jesus for you. More commands. Rejoice, pray, give thanks, why? This is God's will for you. How do I know God's will for my life? Well, here it is, what more do you need? Is what you are pursuing good for you and for all? Go ahead!

Verse 19-22: Do not quench the Spirit. Do not despise prophecies. Test all things; hold fast what is good. Abstain from every form of evil.

This is serious stuff- do not quench the Spirit. Now what does he mean by that? Well, we can be so dulled in our heart and mind that we do not even recognize the Holy Spirit in our lives anymore.

Did you ever get a notion to do something outrageous, outrageously good? Like, I think I ought to tell that person about Jesus- or, you're driving down the road and think, I ought to stop in and visit Bill. And what happens? You are able to put that thought out of your mind ... fill it with something else to do.

Well, practice does not make perfect, that's not true. Practice does not perfect, it makes permanent. If you practice poorly you will do poorly, permanently, or at least until you begin to practice properly. If you ignore the Holy Spirit telling you to do something outrageously wonderful for Christ, then you will be able to ignore the Spirit, quench Him. Don't do it, says Paul!

Do not despise prophecies. Test all things; hold fast what is good. Abstain from every form of evil.

It's another interesting word that Paul uses for prophecies, here. We normally use the word, preaching, and in the New Testament, the word was most times used to mean preaching from the Old Testament. Interesting isn't it that the church needs to be told to not despise preaching.

Test all things; hold fast what is good. In today's English we call this discernment.

And here is the big one: Abstain from every form of evil. Stay away from it, every appearance, form, figure shape of evil. If you can't discern whether something is good or evil, don't do it. Don't even get near it says Paul, don't even look like you're getting near it.

And now we have Paul's beautiful ending to his letter:

Now may the God of peace Himself sanctify you completely; and may your whole spirit, soul, and body be preserved blameless at the coming of our Lord Jesus Christ. He who calls you *is* faithful, who also will do *it*.

Brethren, pray for us. (One last imperative from Paul, because it all really does begin with prayer.)

Greet all the brethren with a holy kiss.

I charge you by the Lord that this epistle be read to all the holy brethren.

The grace of our Lord Jesus Christ *be* with you. Amen.

Here is your job description church. Let's make sure that we do our jobs well.

# DRAW ME NEARER BLESSED LORD

*Hebrews 10:22*

Sermons are funny things, some are easy to write, some are hard to write, some come to mind on Monday, some not until Saturday afternoon. Those are the toughest ones, Saturday afternoon when the sun is shining and I'd rather be outside.

How does one write sermons? I don't know. I suppose I could give you the Sunday School answer that we should fast and pray and seek the Holy Spirit to guide our thoughts and actions. That sounds so spiritual but isn't that what we all should be doing anyway? Don't quench the Spirit I think I read in the Bible.

Besides that, I have to admit that I believe that there are no inspired writings after the Bible. That may surely cause some authors to feel bad but that is just the way God has done things. Even my writings are not Spirit led, God breathed. If they were they would be part of the Bible.

A sermon may be Holy Spirit inspired but it's not Scripture. No modern writings are ...

Sermons are funny things: sometimes I'll come across a verse or two and think, wow, that will make a good sermon, I've really wondering about that in my own life. Remember I've said many times that I write sermons for things I'm dealing with, I'm thinking about.

Sometimes I'll hear a song and think, yeah, that's what I need, I'll make a sermon out of that. Sometimes other people will say something, just a word or two and I'll pick up that concept and make a sermon out of it because it touched my heart.

This week was a little strange for me: I had been working on a sermon from I Corinthians, reading and re-reading a certain passage, even shared some of it with friends.

But then, my two favorite words, but then I came across an old page of notes from a devotion that my good friend Pastor Kermit shared with the boys about six years ago. Funny isn't it? I always tell students and staff, take good notes, you have no idea how useful they will be in the future.

Six years ago Pastor Kermit Rowe was talking about drawing nearer to God, based on the verse from Hebrews 10:22; "...let us draw near with a true heart in full assurance of faith, having our hearts sprinkled from an evil conscience and our bodies washed with pure water."

Normally I don't like to build sermons from the middle of a sentence but this is important. Drawing nearer to God, is that what we want to do? If not, then what are doing? Let's go and watch television.

Seriously, if we are not growing in our faith, if we have no interest in being closer and closer to God as our lives move forward, then what in the world are we doing? Stay home from church for goodness sake, sleep in, watch Sunday Morning on CBS.

Something that Kermit said six years ago that stuck with me: attitude is more important than process; I <u>want</u> to know God more. Key word being want. If that is not what I want ... church won't help you, nothing will.

God wants His creation to know Him. We read a devotion from Psalms 19 the other day before class:

The heavens declare the glory of God;
And the firmament shows His handiwork.

Day unto day utters speech,
And night unto night reveals knowledge.
*There is* no speech nor language
*Where* their voice is not heard.
Their line (sound) has gone out through all the earth,
And their words to the end of the world.

God has given us the means to draw nearer to Him, He just waits for our attitude to be right, for our hearts to be true, to be clean.

God wants His creation to know Him for two reasons:

A general purpose. What is the general purpose that we should grow nearer to God? It really is quite simple- to glorify Him. So people will say, wow, look at them, they must really be near to the Lord, look at their life!

A specific purpose. God wants us to grow nearer to Him for the specific purpose of service. Fanny Crosby's song *Draw Me Nearer*, verse 2: consecrate me now to thy service Lord. Does God use people distant from Him for service? Can we build the Kingdom without knowing the King, in a closer and closer way? Can Kingdom builders have unclean hearts? Untrue motives? Why would you want to try?

And what happens when we are drawn closer and closer to God for the purpose of service? He is glorified still.

Alright, while attitude is better than process there are some things we need to know to grow closer to God.

We need the right attitude we know, and that attitude is a humble spirit. A humble spirit is the right attitude about my ability and the right attitude about God's ability. Remember what Jesus said, without me, you can do nothing? I think that He meant that we can do nothing.

Look at Isaiah chapter 66:1-2

Thus says the Lord:

"Heaven *is* My throne,
And earth *is* My footstool.
Where *is* the house that you will build Me?
And where *is* the place of My rest?
For all those *things* My hand has made,
And all those *things* exist,"
Says the Lord.
"But on this *one* will I look:
On *him who is* poor and of a contrite spirit,
And who trembles at My word.

Over time have we forgotten who the Lord is, and who we are?

Heaven is his throne and the earth his footstool. God is bigger than anything we can imagine, he made all these things, they are nothing to God.

But on this one thing He pays attention to, the person who has is poor and of a contrite spirit, who trembles at his word. In other words, a person who is humble, humble before the Lord.

How many of us tremble at His word? It's not the American thing to do I guess. We're fiercely independent people. Of course we're Christians we're from Ohio aren't we?

That is just what the Pharisees told Jesus, of course we're godly people we are descendants of Abraham. And what did He say? That really does not matter, check your attitude, go back and read Isaiah folks, God seeks out those who are humble, who know Him and know their place, and tremble at His word. He is talking to us here, not pagans, not atheists, but to people who claim to know Him but do not show it by their attitude and actions.

Second thing that we need to draw closer to God is a life of integrity, and reputation. Pastor Kermit said it this way: when I live my life the right way, that gets me right to hear from God. Hmm, sounds like the old don't squelch the Spirit sermon.

I think Peter says it best. I Peter 3:

And who *is* he who will harm you if you become followers of what is good? But even if you should suffer for righteousness' sake, *you are* blessed. "And do not be afraid of their threats, nor be troubled." But sanctify the Lord God in your hearts, and always *be* ready to *give* a defense to everyone who asks you a reason for the hope that is in you, with meekness and fear; having a good conscience, that when they defame you as evildoers, those who revile your good conduct in Christ may be ashamed. For *it is* better, if it is the will of God, to suffer for doing good than for doing evil.

Verse 16 again: having a good conscience, when they defame you, talk bad about you as an evildoer, when they insult your good behavior in Christ, even to the point of calling it evil, they will be ashamed. Because they really find nothing in your behavior to bring anything against you. Are we living our lives that way? no one can bring a charge against us? Not one that is real anyway.

One other point that goes with a life of integrity is confession and repentance. Do we understand the difference? Confession usually comes with being caught, repentance is a change of heart to change behavior. Saying "my bad' is not repentance. Any confession with the word, 'but' in it is not repentance. Repentance is a sorrow in the heart that I realize the damage I have caused and will make every effort to not do so again!

The third thing we need to know to draw closer to God is this: to understand my position in Christ. When we are saved, we become sons and daughters of the Living God, the One who makes heaven His throne and the earth His footstool. We are joint heirs with Christ, we inherit the kingdom!

Paul explains it this way in Romans 8:

*There is* therefore now no condemnation to those who are in Christ Jesus, who do not walk according to the flesh, but according to the Spirit. For the law of the Spirit of life in Christ Jesus has made me free from the law of sin and death.

Life in Christ has made me Free! Free from the law of sin and death! No more under the law! The Ten Commandments no longer apply to me, I'm under the two laws: love the Lord your God with all your heart and soul and mind and love your neighbor as yourself. On these hang all of the law said Jesus.

When I am a child of God the Ten Commandments no longer apply because the Law is in my heart, I no longer want to sin! That does not mean I don't sin, that means I do not want to- be careful here, if your sin doesn't bother you greatly, you may be missing something. You may not be a true child of the King. Many will say to Jesus, Lord, Lord, and what does He say? Depart from me, I never knew you.

Sometimes we can fool people, most times we can even fool ourselves, but you know who you will never fool?

Hebrews 4:12-13

For the word of God *is* living and powerful, and sharper than any two-edged sword, piercing even to the division of soul and spirit, and of joints and marrow, and is a discerner of the thoughts and intents of the heart.

And there is no creature hidden from His sight, but all things *are* naked and open to the eyes of Him to whom we *must give* account.

You will never fool God, He knows where we really stand, and one day, every one of us will give an account. That should make us tremble at His word.

Oh beloved, do you want to draw nearer to God? Are you satisfied where you are in your spiritual life right now? Do you think there is no more to learn, no more to grow? Then please, please search your heart and find out what is wrong. Sounds like the Spirit may be squelched, if He is there at all.

What more to say? James 4:8, Draw near to God and He will draw near to you. Cleanse *your* hands, *you* sinners; and purify *your* hearts, *you* double-minded.

And remember, He's talking to me, to you.

# EVERY SINGLE DAY
# EVERY WORD YOU SAY

*Luke 6:43-45*

You may remember that I've said before that I grew up in the 1970's. We all have some nostalgic thoughts about our childhood from time to time, I like to listen to 1970's music to be sentimental about the good old days.

My wife, Teresa and I were listening to some 70's music one evening and one of us said, you know, the 70's were not really that great. The other one of us said, yeah, I hated the 70's, turn that stuff off. So much for the good old days ...

I heard a pastor shared a story this week about the passing of his brother in law. In his story the pastor said this, "I think of the good he did with family and how they in turn do the Lord's will with many others. It goes on and on. "A good man, out of the good treasure of his heart, brings forth that which is good ... "and it keeps on." What a wonderful eulogy for a real hero of a man.

Now after I read that I had to find out where the verse was that pastor quoted: "A good man, out of the good treasure of his heart, brings forth that which is good." Thanks to the internet I found it in Luke 6, the verses we read earlier.

Now what in the world does 1970's rock and roll have to do with Luke chapter 6? Well, I was immediately reminded of that song by the Police, *Every Breath You Take.*

I had to look up the lyrics to be sure I remembered it right:

Every breath you take
Every move you make
Every bond you break
Every step you take
I'll be watching you

Every single day
Every word you say
Every game you play
Every night you stay
I'll be watching you

There it is in the second verse: every single day, every word you say: A good man out of the good treasure of his heart brings forth good; and an evil man out of the evil treasure of his heart brings forth evil. For out of the abundance of the heart his mouth speaks.

Out of the abundance of the heart, what is most in our hearts is what comes out of our mouths. Every word you say, every game you play.

There is a parallel story to the words of Jesus here in Luke, it's Matthew 12:33-37. Matthew records it just a little differently, a little bit harsher I think. Jesus did not pull any punches when He spoke and Matthew makes sure to get that point across.

Look at verses 36-37 again. Every idle word will be given an account, by your words you will be justified, by your words you will be condemned. Wow! Does Jesus mean what He just said here? I've heard a lot of sermons scaring us not to speak idle words, because we will have to account for them at the judgment day.

Let's start at the beginning of the paragraph and see if we can makes sense out of what Jesus is saying here. He has just been accused of casting out demons by the power of evil and He has explained the unpardonable sin of blaspheme against the Holy Spirit- let's pick things up in verse 33.

This is an agricultural society, they understand the reference to grafting here- make the tree good, or make it bad, there is no in between. Is you is or is you aint? There is no sitting on the fence with Jesus.

Verse 34: Jesus calls them a brood of vipers! I told you that Jesus is a little more harsh here in Matthew, brood of vipers, he calls the Pharisees, the religious folk, the church folk. Brood of vipers-

How can any good word come from a brood of vipers? Their hearts are naturally and basically evil, an abundance of evil as Jesus alludes to. Evil comes out of their mouths because that's what's in their hearts. That's the way it works, as a man thinketh in his heart, so is he, we read in the Proverbs.

Verse 35: here is that verse again, a good man, and compare him with an evil man.

The heart is the treasure says Matthew Henry in his commentary, and the words and the actions are the produce of that treasure. The love of Christ dominates a good man and brings good treasure.

But where the love of the world reigns in the heart, an evil man continually brings forth evil. Out of the abundance of the heart the mouth speaks- whatever comes out of our mouths agrees with what is in our hearts. No matter what we pretend to be, our words eventually give us away- our words give away what is really in our hearts.

Now don't get excited and become a word inspector, a good man may possibly drop a bad word, and a wicked man may use a good word, but it is the abundance of the heart that gives us away. What is generally thought is generally said by all of us.

The general character of a person filled with the Holy Spirit shows in their language, speaking: grace, comfort, forgiveness, encouragement, truth; uplifting the Body of Christ and building on the Kingdom for the glory of God.

Just a thought, what is the tool we foundationally use to build the Kingdom? Yes, the Bible, but how do folks know to read the Bible? Yes, the Holy Spirit but how do folks know when they have a conviction of the Spirit or indigestion?

It really is simpler than we think: we have to tell people, we have to talk, we have to use words. We speak to tell people about Jesus.

Yes, yes behaviors matter, but all the good behaviors in the world can be ruined with one evil word. And it works the other way too- all the glorious words in the world can be ruined by bad behaviors.

Back to what Jesus said- out of the abundance of the heart the mouth speaks, your words will eventually give you away, give away what is truly in your heart.

James wrote, "If anyone among you thinks he is religious, and does not bridle his tongue but deceives his own heart, this one's religion *is* useless." 1:26

"Does a spring send forth fresh *water* and bitter from the same opening? Can a fig tree, my brethren, bear olives, or a grapevine bear figs? Thus no spring yields both salt water and fresh." James 3:11-12

These are rhetorical questions, in other words, James does not expect us to answer, we already know the answer, the whole world knows the answer! Of course not, either you is or you aint. Fresh water or bitter? Figs or olives? Grapes or figs? Salt water or fresh? You know what is in your heart and it shows out of our mouths said Jesus.

Every idle word will be given account on the judgment day. Now before we get all excited and begin worrying about whether we have spoken any idle words that we will have to admit to on judgment day- relax. He is talking to the religious folks, the Pharisees, the people who all of the common folks looked up to as the saintly religious leaders. The ones who thought that they were especially blessed by God- they thought they were saved, but they were not.

They thought that they had God's favor, "I've sat in this pew every Sunday since 1953, of course I'm saved," people. But they are only fooling themselves.

Hey, another 1970's song: Styx, *The Angry Young Man*. "You see the world through your cynical eyes ... You're fooling yourself if you don't believe it, you're killing yourself if you don't believe it," for all of eternity! Literally!

So, relax born again believers, only those who Jesus says depart from me I never knew you are the ones who face judgement of every idle word. The ones fooling themselves. We are covered by the Blood, no commendation, no judgement required, it's been taken care of by Jesus.

Now here is something to think about: As biblical counselors, we are trained to look for certain issues, behaviors that trouble people- biblical counseling goes so far as to say, the people that you are counseling may not be saved. They may pretend that they are, they may be highly religious, they may be in church every Sunday since the 1950's, but they are really not saved.

See verse 37 again: by your words you will be justified, your words will prove what is really, really in your heart, and by your words you will be condemned. Do our words prove whether we are saved or not? Seems to be what Jesus is saying here. of course, He has the advantage, He can see your heart. It's all the rest of us that can hear your words ...

Oh beloved, don't fool yourself any longer. What you say shows where your heart is. Don't go another day without being sure of your Salvation in Jesus. You don't want to give an account of every idle word at judgement day- I know I don't.

Today is the day of salvation wrote the Apostle Paul. Are you fooling yourself and you don't believe it? you are not fooling anyone else, especially Jesus.

I have to admit something: *Every Breath You Take* was not released by the Police until 1983, it was not a 1970's song. Funny, I don't remember listening to music in the 1980's but I must have heard it somewhere … next, we'll try to tie in some Boston or Kansas into the lesson.

# GIMME, GIMME

II *Corinthians 8:1-15*

My daughter, son-in-law, and grandkids bought a new Bible for me last birthday: The American Patriot's Bible. Seems like they have Bibles for every special interest group these days doesn't it? Have you been to a Christian book store lately?

Beginners Bible, bedtime story Bible, the teen Bible, the creative journaling Bible, the bi-polar Bible has just the Psalms; no I just made that one up ... But you see my point.

There's nothing wrong with all of that- the Patriot's Bible has interesting stories in it outside of Scripture. I was reading this story about R.G. Le Tourneau earlier this week. I was familiar with his name and some of his inventions but this is interesting: he is called the father of the modern earth moving industry. He invented the bulldozer, earth mover, cranes, wagons, dump beds, even mobile sea platforms for oil drilling. During WWII he and his company produced 70% of the army's earthmoving machinery.

I learned about R.G. Le Tourneau when my daughter Shelley was in high school and looking at Christian Colleges. R.G. founded a college in Longview Texas, Le Tourneau University. We never visited the college but interestingly enough the company I worked for owned the newspaper in those days in Longview Texas.

One of the things that interested me in the story about R.G. Le Tourneau was the establishment of the Le Tourneau Foundation, funded by 90% of his personal salary. Now I know what you're thinking- if you make $10 million a year and give away 90% that still makes you a millionaire every year. To that I say, so what? If you make $10,000 per year and give away $9,000 you still make $1,000 per year; more than most of the world! If I remember right, the widow gave all that she had in Luke 21, two mites.

Le Tourneau was famous for his generosity. He always said that money came in faster than he could give it away. "I shovel it out," he said, "and God shovels it back in, but God has a bigger shovel."

I have already been thinking often of giving and generosity the past month or so. I heard a pastor say recently that he always apologizes before his gives he annual sermon on tithing. Why? Not why do you apologize but why do you so strongly feel the need to give your annual sermon on tithing? Seriously, what is that all about?

Honestly, I will admit that I have been so tired of hearing about money being argued and discussed and focused upon that ... well, I don't know what. I am just fed up with it. Now again I know what you're thinking, Jesus talked more about money than He did heaven and hell. At least that's what the pastor I mentioned earlier told me. In Malachi is the only place that God says to test Him by giving money. And to that I use my best argument once again: so what? I know all of those Sunday School answers, so what?

Solomon was the smartest and richest person the world has ever seen and he said it was all vanity, emptiness. We are not going to take a nickel with us, and who knows, maybe a fool will inherit all we hold so dear here in the flesh. (Solomon said that too)

There is no doubt in my mind that Satan gets us so focused on money issues and arguments that we forget what the real focus ought to be. R.G. Le Tourneau's life verse was familiar: Matthew 6:33. But, seek first the kingdom of God and His righteousness, and all these things will be added unto you. Kingdom, righteousness, boy if we were to seek those things first ... my guess is all that we need would be added unto us. What do you think?

So, back to II Corinthians chapter 8 to see what Paul has to say to the church there in Corinth. He points out how generous the churches of Macedonia were: Philippi, Thessalonica, and Berea, maybe others. Even though they were in deep poverty and trial of affliction, they gave freely willingly, beyond their ability, they were super generous people, urgently wanting their gift to be received and used.

Look at verse 5: but, they first gave themselves to the Lord ...

Does that not sound like first they were seeking the kingdom and righteousness? And everything else was added unto them. Where do good gifts come from anyway? What did James say?

They gave beyond their ability, where do you think that above and beyond came from? The lottery? 50/50 drawing at the Lion's Club? No! from God. Verse 5 says so: then to us by the will of God.

Verse 7: you abound in everything, faith, speech, knowledge, diligence and your love for us! Well then, abound in this grace also! What grace? Giving!

Notice the order here.

Faith, without faith it is impossible to please Him ...

Speech, do you have faith? Say so! When our faith is big we can't help but tell.

Knowledge, builds on the faith and speech, I want to know God more and more. I want the Word, I want to grow.

Diligence, they walked the talk. They did what they said and knew to do. See some big talkers and knowers don't have diligence, but the Corinthians did! They were people of action.

And in their love; they loved Paul and his companions and the work of the Lord. I know how much easier it is to pick apart our Christian leaders than it is to love them ...

Paul takes the next few sentences to tell the Corinthians simply: it's good to copy what the Macedonian churches have done. For they were copying what the Lord Jesus Christ did for us. For our sakes, he became poor that through His poverty we might become rich. Through His sacrifice on the Cross, we have eternal life! Let that sink in for a minute. Like R.G. Le Tourneau said, you can't out give God and he didn't just mean money, he meant Salvation!

Verse 10 and 11- Paul encourages the Corinthians to complete the project they began a year ago. It is to your advantage! Again, it's not enough to say you'll do something, it's not enough to have good intentions, it's not enough to have a great desire to do so, you must also complete the doing of it says Paul.

Remember what James said about faith without works? Dead. In the original Greek that word means dead, absolutely dead, completely dead.

Verse 12, first there is a willing mind. Generosity is of the heart and mind, and it is accepted according to what you have, not what you don't have. Let that sink in for a minute. God measures the gift according to what you have, not what you don't have.

That beloved is a serious, serious concept. We are measured by what we have, not what we don't have. Well, I can't give millions like R.G. Le Tourneau did. My famous argument again: so what?

God does accept your gifts by what you do not have, millions, but by what you do have. The widow in Luke gave two mites, more than all the rich folks combined. She wasn't judged for what she did not have, she was judged for what she did have, and she gave all. Wow- suddenly that story in Luke seems so much more important to me, she gave all. Do you know how tough it was to be a widow in that culture? She truly had the focus on seeking the kingdom and righteousness.

Verse 13-15 is a God math lesson. Others eased and you burdened? No, give from your abundance, the problem is we don't recognize our abundance. And they give back, reciprocity we call that, and all needs are met. It's a win-win situation.

But here is the point for us: back to verse 7. If we don't abound first in faith, which shows in our speech, which grows in our knowledge, which is practically applied in our diligence to do what we say, and shows in our love, then forget it. Put your money away, God doesn't want it or need it.

See generosity is first a blessing to the giver, then to the getter, again, it's a win-win. But like I said earlier, there are a lot of folks with knowledge and speech who don't have faith diligence or love, so there are a lot of folks who write checks that don't have any of these: faith, speech, knowledge, diligence or love.

As Paul Simon sang: "now who do, who do you think you're foolin'?" She loves me like a rock, Paul Simon, 1973. You knew I could reference a 1970's song somehow ...

Seriously, if your giving finds others eased and you burdened like verse 13, then something is wrong. Not your giving but your faith, your speech, your knowledge, your diligence and your love is somehow out of kilter. Plainly, if you are not seeing the return on investment that God is promising, then please, please check your heart. Your faith just might be dead, completely dead.

Today is the day of Salvation wrote Paul, if you are not completely positive about Jesus then don't let this day go by without knowing that Jesus Christ is your Savior. It's just too dangerous out there without knowing that Heaven is for sure.

# THE SECRET PLACE

*Matthew 6:8-13*

I had the chance to talk to an old friend this week for several hours. If you knew my friend Larry, you'll know why I said for several hours; no one just talks to Larry for a few minutes. That fellow can talk.

Larry and his family are such solid Christians, he really is a joy to talk to so you really don't mind spending time with him. It's easy to lose track of time talking with Larry.

Larry understands that everything begins with prayer and he asked me if I would pray for a young man in his church. The little fellow is only six years old, his name is Barrett, and he has liver cancer- almost always fatal. And of course I told him that I would pray for Barrett.

All that made me think a lot about prayer this week. One foundation of prayer that I try to always do: if I tell someone I will pray, then I expect to really do so. I know how easy it is to say, why sure I'll pray and then walk away and forget all about it. That's another reason I always say, take good notes. You can tell if I'm going to do something in that I write it down- if I do not write it down, I am not going to do it.

Then I came across this quote by a fellow named Samuel Zwemer:

*"Prayer is self-discipline. The effort to realize the presence and power of God stretches the sinews of the soul and hardens muscles. To pray is to grow in grace. To tarry in the presence of the King leads to new loyalty and devotion on the*

*part of the faithful subjects. Christian character grows in the secret place of prayer."* -Samuel M. Zwemer

That's a very nice quote but I'm not really sure about that self-discipline stuff. I don't have it. If I relied on my self-discipline for my prayer life I'll tell you how much I would pray: none.

See we like to think it's all about us and to some degree it is but we need to think differently about this. Look at Matthew chapter 6 and start at verse 5. The hypocrites, the religious folks, the Pharisees love to pray standing in the synagogues, the churches, and on the street corners so people can see them and hear them. These boys are extremely self-disciplined about prayer, they don't miss a lick, my grandpa used to say.

They are way more disciplined than I am, hope that does not disappoint you too much.

I read an article this week about how we think, how we act as people, our routines. The author talked about our morning routine: we get up, turn on the television to hear the news or the weather, turn on the coffee maker and on and on. And the point he was making was this: is the first thing that we do is turn on the weather and news, or spend some time with the Omniscient Creator of the universe?

See here is the point: we are going to spend time with what is important to us; it's not about self-discipline, that's for the hypocrites, it's about what we love. Do we love the news? Do we love the weather? Do we love coffee? That is where we will spend our time, energy and focus, no matter how much self-discipline we think that we have.

The article that had the Samuel Zwemer quote went to ask these questions:

Where do you live?

Where do you sleep?

Where do you eat?

When and *where* do you pray?

Most would respond, "Over food" — "with my kids" — "in church". Common answers. And good answers.

I don't think that's enough. I don't mean not enough prayer, not enough questions. I would go further to ask:

What do you love? That is the most basic question to answer all of these others.

It really isn't that hard: do you love your home? Of course, so you'll spend a lot of time there.

Do you love your family? Then you will spend a lot of time with them. You don't spend much time with folks that you don't like do you? That would be sadistic now wouldn't it.

Do you love your bank account? You will spend a lot of time checking it.

You can see the point here can't you? How often have you heard me say, what are thinking about when you aren't thinking about anything? Really we spend that time thinking about the things that we love don't we?

Back to Matthew 6, verse 6:

Jesus talked about a place of prayer that really mattered to Him — the "secret place". A place of solitude where He would often withdraw into privacy and spiritual intimacy with His Father. Do you think that Jesus spent time and energy with those that He loved, starting with the Father?

It is interesting that Jesus used the religious people of His day as a warning about prayer. They loved to pray in public. For show. With loud voices. Out of self-discipline and duty and pride. Jesus made it clear that being seen by others was their reward.

Let that sink in for a minute: when we bring prayer requests is it because we love the Lord our God with all of hearts and souls and minds and we love our neighbors as ourselves? Or is it out of some kind duty, pride and gossip? I've got the news on so and so and you need to hear it!

Remember what I told Larry, yes, I will pray for Barrett? And I said that means that I will really pray for Barrett? Well, here's how to tell if your heart is really concerned for a prayer request or are you just gossiping? Are you praying for what you are bringing to the church? That may be a hard question to answer.

Our time and energy is spent on what we love. If we are not praying for whatever we are bringing up, then we are not spending our time and energy there and obviously we do not love whomever ... that just makes it gossip.

Back to Matthew 6:6. With encouraging direction Jesus gives us instruction, "But when you pray, go into your room and shut the door and pray to your Father who is in secret".

The "secret place". Where God abides. Where He sees into our hearts and minds. The room in which God is in touch with the things we think go unnoticed, but matter deeply to Him and us.

And by the way, Jesus added — "your Father who sees in secret will reward you." Sowing in the secret place of prayer, reaps God's rewards. Do you believe that? Are you collecting the rewards?

The writer of the Samuel Zwemer quote went on to say this: 'You can tell people who pray in secret. Their countenance shines with the very Glory of God. They have a humble boldness. A gentle strength. The mind of Christ.

But too often the pace of life has paralyzed the power of our prayers. We have relegated our "quiet time" to spiritual fast food, micro-waved on the fly. A quick "Bless me Lord" as we head off to bed or into a day of the unknown.

Finding time to pray, much less a "secret place" is hard to do with the press of the world, and the pressures of our much-too-busy lives.'

Again those are nice words and thoughts but they miss the one big point: we do find time to spend with what we love. It is not a time problem, it is not a self-discipline problem, it is a heart problem! Turn off the television, you have all day to check the weather and your bank account.

Get to that space in life where it is just you and God. It is private. Separate. Alone. No show and tell there. No flowery words meant to impress anybody. No gossip. Just raw, direct intimacy with our Creator. What is really, really on our hearts.

In the secret place, it's God and you.

It will turn your life around.

# THE MEANING OF WORSHIP

*Psalm 147*

My goodness I never realized how many different opinions there are within the church about the style and culture of what we call the 'worship service' especially opinions about the raising of hands. Wow, can people get hung up on the silliest things, and what impresses me most is that everyone has Scripture of some sort to back up their idea.

This is called proof texting, folks. Here is how it works: we have a preconceived idea, maybe it's how we grew up, maybe it matches our personality, maybe we read about it or dreamed it. Then we find Scripture verses or bits of verses to verify that idea. We've all done it; you know just what I mean.

Here is a personal example: I grew in a church that never, I mean never would sing a song if it wasn't in the hymnal. And if you even suggested that someone might raise a hand in singing or in prayer, you stood a chance of being banished. Well maybe not that but you would certainly get a stern lecture from the elders.

And they were elders, not deacons; deacon was separate office lower than the elders.

If there was any special music you would not, I repeat, you would not clap or show any kind of appreciation for that person. Appreciation was reserved specially for God; we were to be no respecters of people.

Now I could go on and on but the point is this, I thought this was how church was supposed to be done. It wasn't until years later that I discovered that I had grown up in a church that had mostly dead all day ... for years actually. Not because of their culture, but because of their attitudes.

Here is one more interesting example. Guess what translation of the Bible the church I grew up in used exclusively: King James and King James only.

Romans 12:1 is a good example: I beseech you therefore, brethren, by the mercies of God, that ye present your bodies a living sacrifice, holy, acceptable unto God, which is your reasonable service.

Now we are really familiar with that verse, heard many sermons about it over the years, I've given sermons about it over the years. But as part of my doctoral training, I had to show my proficiency in New Testament Greek. Not having much proficiency in New Testament Greek I had to fake it ... no, really, I can read enough Greek to cause trouble, and guess what? In Greek that verse does not exactly mean what I always thought it meant.

Here is a closer translation: Therefore I urge you, brethren, by the mercies of God, to present your bodies a living and holy sacrifice, acceptable to God, which is your spiritual service of worship. Did you hear the difference? This verse is about worship- those last two words in Greek mean spiritual service, of worship.

Well of course! It makes much better sense to me now, therefore, because all that Paul outlined in the previous chapter, by the mercies of God, present your bodies a living sacrifice, acceptable. Well, what is sacrifice? A form of worship! My whole life, my living sacrifice is one of worship. This is my spiritual service of worship.

I know that when we hear the word "worship," most of us think of the songs we sing every Sunday morning. But we need to understand one thing: In and of itself, music has nothing to do with worship. We can be listening to and singing songs (even Christian songs) all day long and be partaking in nothing that resembles worship to God.

We also think that music has a way of jump-starting our worship to God, which also is not really true. Music is not the beginning of worship, it is the end of it. When we sing to God and play music to him, it is merely the expression of the worship that is already in our hearts.

So when we go to church on Sunday morning to worship God, it's not what we do that's important—it's our hearts. Isaiah 29:13 says, "These people come near to me with their mouth and honor me with their lips, but their hearts are far from me." What we sing and what we do matter far less in comparison with where our hearts are. Are we worshiping God with our hearts?

However, this leaves the question of how we express this heart worship. It is foolish for us to think that we can be worshiping God with our hearts and our emotions will remain unaffected. It is clear when you read Scripture, especially the Psalms, that our emotions are part of our worship.

If you want to know how to express those emotions, look to the words of David. Time and again, he pleads with Israel to "clap your hands!" and "shout to God with a voice of triumph!" He tells us to "dance with joy before the Lord" and to "praise Him with the tambourine and lyre." You can almost feel a holy frustration in his writing where he cries out to his people saying, "Don't you guys know who God is? Shout to Him! Sing to Him! Dance for Him! Praise Him, praise Him, praise Him!"

The fact of the matter is that we are emotional beings and, although our emotions can be misleading if we rely on them entirely, they can be amazing expressions of our worship to God. When we truly understand the Gospel and are dwelling on true and biblically sound thoughts of God, our hearts will respond to those thoughts with feelings, as well.

But it's important to remember that an emotional expression of worship is only godly when it is rooted in a proper understanding of who God is.

John 4:24 says, "God is spirit, and his worshipers must worship in spirit and in truth." Worship is a spiritual event, and true worship comes from the heart. If our worship is not heartfelt, it doesn't matter what posture or expression of worship we use. If our worship is from the heart, God accepts our worship. We call church the worship service where we can proclaim through prayer and praise our adoration and thankfulness to Him and what He has done for us.

True worship is felt inwardly and then is expressed through our actions. "Worshiping" out of obligation is displeasing to God and is completely in vain. He can see through all the hypocrisy, and He hates it. A good example is the story of Cain and Abel. Abel's worship is accepted, Cain's is not. We can argue all day about why that was so, but the matter remains as fact.

True worship is God-centered worship. People tend to get caught up in where they should worship, what music they should sing in worship, and how their worship looks to other people. Focusing on these things misses the point.

Jesus tells us that true worshipers will worship God in spirit and in truth. This means we worship from the heart and the way God has designed. Worship can include praying, reading God's Word with an open heart, singing, participating in communion, and serving others. It is not limited to one act, but is done properly when the heart and attitude of the person are in the right place.

True worship is not confined to what we do in church or open praise (although these things are both good, and we are told in the Bible to do them). True worship is the acknowledgment of God and all His power and glory in everything we do. The highest form of praise and worship is obedience to Him and His Word. To do this, we must know God; we cannot be ignorant of Him. Worship is to glorify and exalt God—to show our loyalty and admiration to our Father.

So, what do raised hands signify? For one, raised hands are symbolic of our dependence on someone else. Raising hands during worship can be similar to children who lift their hands to be picked up, comforted, protected, or carried: "I stretch out my hands to you; my soul thirsts for you like a parched land" Psalm 143:6. So raised hands in worship may suggest a reaching out for God's presence, blessing, comfort, or strength.

This week look through the Psalms and see King David's expressions of worship. Remember, he is called a man after God's own heart, I think he may have a thing or two to tell us about worship.

O clap your hands all ye people, shout unto God with the voice of triumph, David said. But most importantly, it has to come from your heart. Nothing else matters.

Besides looking at worship in the Psalms this week, think about things that we do or don't do not because Scripture back it up somehow, but because that's the way we've always done it.

And one last point- you know where we almost see the raising of hands in Scripture? Not singing, but in prayer. That's a good one to start with, why do we fold our hands or whatever we do? Why don't raise our hands in prayer?

There is a lot to think about this week ...

# JESUS, WHAT FOR?

*John 6:35-40*

Sometimes life gets frustrating, doesn't it? things don't quite go the way we think that they go, people don't do the things that we think that they should do. Look around us; we wonder why God doesn't see fit to accept our ideas? I don't know, it's frustrating.

This week one of our friends was talking about family and said something like, it's really frustrating to try to help people that really don't seem to want help. Welcome to ministry.

I love it when folks come for advice or counsel and when they get it they say, oh I could never do that, I could never stop doing that. Well, what did you ask for then?

Not too long ago I talked by phone to a father having a lot of trouble with his son and looking at our school. He wanted to know what kind of television we watched and I told him none. We really do not watch television. Well, my son could never come there he said, he's got to watch television ... really? Really?

I think we get just as frustrated we share Jesus with friends and family and other folks and they just shrug it off. I know what we think when that happens: 1. We feel the rejection, we think it's us, that we failed someway or somehow, 2. We don't dare say it but we think, 'well, just go to hell then'. It's incomprehensible why anybody in the world would reject the free gift of Salvation, isn't it?

Well, first of all, it's not us, you, me that is being rejected, it's God. And, God does not send anybody to hell, that is strictly their choice and there is absolutely nothing that anyone else can do about it. You can lead a horse to water, but you cannot make him drink ... is true.

I love what our counselor always says: the good news is that it's up to you; the bad news is that it's up to you. We cannot control other people no matter what. Which I think adds to our frustration. I told one of our parents this week, sorry, but everything you learned in college was a lie, behavior modification does not work. There are some people who just do not care about rewards and/or punishment, stop wasting your time. If reward and punishment worked then everyone would be saved!

I ran out of books to read last week so I started a series by Oswald Chambers. His claim to fame, if you remember was that he wrote a famous devotional called *My Utmost for His Highest.* I always thought that most of his work was boring.

But, having nothing else in the house to read I picked up book one of a series he wrote- fell asleep on the couch every night. He didn't disappoint me, it was boring.

But then I came across a chapter that really got my attention, called Following God. Preparing for my pre-bedtime nap on the couch, Oswald Chambers wrote something that made me pay attention. He said Christ didn't come to save men's souls ... huh? He said Christ came to show His obedience to the Father, to do the Father's will and by His obedience, obedience to the point of death, even death of the cross, wrote Paul in Philippians, and by his obedience men may be saved!

If we are truly followers of Christ, imitators of Jesus, then our duty is obedience, not evangelism.

Now wait just a minute pastor, that sounds like heresy ... we know about the Great Commission and sharing Jesus and taking as many people to Heaven with us as we can- goodness, even I have preached and written on that concept. How in the world can you say that our duty is not evangelism?

(Them's hanging words ...)

And did you say that Jesus didn't come to save men's souls? What was the name of liberal college where you studied theology?

Before you get out the tar and feathers, look at the passage we read in John 6 again. Are you spiritually hungry? Jesus is the Bread of Life! Are you spiritually dry, thirsty? Jesus is the Living Water!

Verse 36: You have seen but still do not believe! Oh my, does that sound familiar at all? You have seen with your own eyes, you know the truth and still you do not believe. You can lead a horse to water ...

We get frustrated when people don't accept Jesus, when they don't take the simplest advice even after they ask for it. Think about this- these folks rejected Jesus directly. They had seen the miracles and still did not believe!

Verse 37: But, the ones who do come to Me are safe forever.

Verse 38-39: Here it is, I have come to do the will of my Father. Jesus will be obedient to the Father, even to death on the cross.

And remember what he prayed in the Garden of Gethsemane? Not My will but Your will be done! Jesus came to do the will of the Father, to model complete obedience, even death.

Verse 40: and this is the will of the Father: everyone who sees the Son ...

The free gift of salvation and everlasting life. Some will accept it and Jesus will make sure of it. He will not lose one, not one.

Okay, I think I get it, but what does this all have to do with my frustration at people? People who do not accept the free gift, people who come to me for help and then reject it, even if the solution is something so simple, and free in the case of being saved?

In the chapter and book I was reading Oswald Chambers said something like this: it is so easy for us to get so caught up in the winning of souls for eternity that we forget just what the mission is. There you go again pastor with more heresy ...

Can you find any place in Scripture where Jesus was disappointed when He was rejected? He surely was frustrated by the disciples a couple of times but never disappointed. He knew the mission. We just read it: I have come down from Heaven not to do my own will, but the will of Him who sent me.

The mission is to do the Father's will. You see we get so caught up in winning souls, we get so caught up in ministry that we forget what the mission is, who the mission is.

We get so caught up in helping people, in being that good servant that we forget the prime directive (for you Star Trek fans). That's why we are frustrated! We feel like we are beating our heads against the wall because we are! There cannot be peace and joy in our lives unless we make the mission the first thing in lives.

Listen closely: And very simply, the mission is to do what Jesus did, the will of the Father. And to know the Father's will we first have to know the Father. I know what some people are thinking, I am saturated with prayer and Bible verses and living a holy life, and confessing when I sin and on and on ... what are you talking about?

We've put other people before God, I tell you plainly. I am more concerned with serving, with making sure people know the Gospel than I am with knowing the Gospel maker. I've made Christian service an idol! Let that sink in for a minute.

Here's the answer, here is the way to get life back on the right track. Here is the way to peace in our lives rather than frustration when rejected.

Here is the way to joy in impossible circumstances: Love the Lord your God with all of your heart and soul and mind. That's how to know to do the will of Father, to know the Father is to love Him, to grow in Him, to live in Him.

I know, I really only have one or two different lessons but that really is how simple all of this is ... a child can understand it!

Love the Lord your God with all of your heart, and soul and mind. And the second is like it: love your neighbor as yourself. We've had those backwards the last few months.

Today, in my life, I'm turning them around. I'm putting the Father back at number one, just like Jesus's example.

Feeling less frustrated already ...

# I KNOW WHAT YOU'RE THINKING

*(it comes out of your mouth)*
II *Corinthians 10:1-6*

A good friend gave me an interesting book to read a few weeks ago, *Hung by the Tongue* it's called. You can tell it's an oldie by the author's haircut in his picture. And by how wide his tie is and his polyester suit.

Now, I'm not making fun- I kept the book for an extra week or so to read it again and again. There are some really intriguing ideas that the author, Francis Martin has here- some of them I felt like, yeah, I knew that. I'm glad somebody agrees with me.

Ever read a book or have a thought and somebody verifies it? Even when it goes against what we call conventional wisdom? We should start calling conventional wisdom secular wisdom maybe? Because it usually is not all that wise ...

If I were to sum up his book in a short thought I would say, words are powerful, be careful what you say because it shows what is in your heart, and that shows where your thoughts are.

Proverbs 18:21 says that, "Death and life are in the power of the tongue, and those who love it will eat its fruit."

Death and life are in the power of the tongue- let that sink for a minute. How is a death sentence carried out? By the spoken word. How are hearts broken, lives shattered, emotions crushed? All by the power of the tongue. We know that the Book of James has a lot to say about the tongue and words- did you think he was spoofing? He writes about putting bits in horse's mouths, ships turned by rudders, and forest fires started by the tongue.

Listen carefully to James 3:6: And the tongue is a fire, the *very* world of iniquity; the tongue is set among our members as that which defiles the entire body, and sets on fire the course of *our* life, and is set on fire by hell.

I think that James is pretty serious about the tongue, eh?

It defiles the entire body, the tongue? It sets on fire the course of our life, really? The whole course of our life is determined by the tongue?

I can think of two times in my life that the entire course of my future was changed by my words: When I asked, Teresa, will you marry me? And, Jesus, please forgive me, I accept your free gift of Salvation!

Those words changed my life and my eternity.

What do you think? Are our words really that powerful or what? Remember what the police officer said the last time that you were arrested? You have the right to remain silent ... that's how powerful words are- they can and will be used against you.

Hung by the tongue, it has a catchy title doesn't it? Now really, how many times have we been hung by our own tongues? When was the last time you thought: oh, I wish I hadn't said that? A few minutes ago?

Ok, back to some points that Francis Martin made in his book.

-Spiritual Laws cannot be broken he says. That's a good foundation to start with no matter what we are studying: Spiritual Laws cannot be broken, if God says it, it is it.

-What is in the heart comes out of the mouth. You know that concept is in Scripture several times, it's a Spiritual Law, we just do not seem to believe it. What is in my heart comes out of my mouth, not the other way around.

For instance, if I say something mean, or sarcastic, or gossip, something that really hurts someone, or something behind their back, that came right from my heart. Your words come right from your heart ... think about that for a minute.

- Another point from Francis Martin, and I love this one. Satan cannot read our thoughts, he can only attack our minds. He cannot read our thoughts but he sure can hear our words, and anything you say can and will be used against you, guaranteed. Don't give him ammunition.

Anybody remember that Sunday School kids song from the 1960's and 1970's? Oh be careful little eyes what you see, oh be careful little ears what you hear, for the Father up above is looking down in love ... that last verse said be careful little tongue what you say!

Funny thing, seeing and hearing are passive activities, they happen to us, what we say is an active event, we do it to others.

Hmmm, I'm liking that right to remain silent better and better all the time.

Ok, we've seen just how powerfully negative our words can be, a world of iniquity said James, defiles the whole body and set on fire by hell. Pretty bleak isn't it? So where is the hope? Only in one place, only in one person can we find hope: Jesus Christ.

Once we are born again, once we have spoken those eternity changing words of repentance and belief, we can and must have the Holy Spirit which then gives us the mind of Christ.

Look back to I Corinthians 2, start at verse 6:

We speak wisdom ...

We speak the wisdom of God ...

That great mystery, that hidden wisdom, revealed in our Lord Jesus Christ! If they had known, they wouldn't have crucified Him!

Verse 10: God revealed this mystery, this hidden wisdom to us through the Holy Spirit.

We cannot speak of what we do not know and we cannot know God without the Holy Spirit, verse 11.

Verse 13: so we speak ... not in man's wisdom, for verse 14 the natural man just does not get it. It's foolishness to unsaved people. No wonder their words are sarcastic, gossipy, mean-spirited; unsaved people still have broken hearts. They need a heart transplant by being born-again.

But verse 15: he who is spiritual ... yet judged by no one.

Now this is really interesting and there are several opinions about what exactly Paul means here. Matthew Henry says that no man, especially a man who is not spiritual, can discern or judge whether the spiritual man speaks truth or not.

Ok, that seems a little complex to me.

Dr. Gromacki says that Paul divides all men into three categories here: natural, spiritual, and carnal. The carnal man is saved but not yielded to the Holy Spirit so he is not in a position to be taught or to judge. He beaves and speaks like an unsaved man. Carnal Christians was a buzz word when Dr. Gromacki wrote his, *New Testament Survey*.

I have to say, I don't know. Are there carnal Christians? Are there saved people who act and behave and speak like the unsaved? I'll tell you this: I wouldn't wait until eternity to find out. Repent! if that's the way you find your tongue working then repent! Change direction and don't count on something that is not real.

I'll tell you what I think and it starts in the Book of Job, Chapter 13.

My favorite verse is Job 13:15, Though he slay me, yet will I trust in him: but I will maintain mine own ways before him.

I will trust in the Lord no matter what, even if I die.

But, there's our word again: I will maintain my ways before Him ... I will argue my actions, my behaviors, my words before Him.

You see, Job's friends have accused him of wrongdoing and suffering because of sin. They have judged Job and found him guilty of, of something. They spend about 38 chapters trying to figure out what he did.

Well, what did Job do to deserve all of the misery he was facing? Nothing, absolutely nothing. He was a righteous and upright man, according to God. And Job knows it- but I will maintain my ways before God, I will even argue that I have done nothing wrong ... because he didn't. No matter how it looked to his friends.

They were not qualified to judge him; he who is spiritual judges all things, yet he himself is judged by no one.

And just in case you aren't convinced about the carnal Christian being a myth, Job goes on: He also shall be my salvation: for an hypocrite shall not come before him.

Back to I Corinthians verse 16 is a rhetorical question, for we have the mind of the Christ.

And if we really have the mind of Christ, then we have a new heart and from that new heart Paul told the Philippians (4:7) Let the peace of God rule in your hearts" and the peace of God changes what comes out of our mouths!

Our tongues are no longer setting the world around us on fire, defiling our whole body, and leading us right to hell like we see in James.

Ephesians 4:29: Let no corrupt communication proceed out of your mouth, but that which is good to the use of edifying, that it may minister grace unto the hearers.

Colossians 4:6: Let your speech be always with grace, seasoned with salt, that ye may know how ye ought to answer every man.

Beloved, if your tongue is not working like these two verses then you don't need a tongue transplant or a bridle, you need a heart transplant!

If you find yourself speaking like a carnal Christian as your normal behavior, then I will tell you frankly, you are not. You really need to check your heart because what is in your heart comes out of your mouth and, Jesus said, "For by your words you will be justified, and by your words you will be condemned."

Search your hearts, know that you are born again.

# STAY THIRSTY, MY FRIENDS

*Psalm 63:1-8*

I've been reading the Book of Job the last several weeks working on a sermon and a Bible lesson or two. Funny thing, I happened to pick up another Oswald Chambers book, this one about Job, and Bible Study magazine last month was almost exclusively about the Book of Job. It really got my attention.

But this week something different happened- it got really hot. Now what in the world does weather that have to do with a lesson on Job? Nothing really, and yet everything. Think about what had happened to Job: he lost everything, everything including his children. He is at the depths of despair; life just doesn't get any worse on this planet than what Job suffered.

From the depths of despair what does Job think? He doesn't blame the government, he doesn't blame bad luck, the weather, his own behavior (because he knows that he is a righteous man), or anything else. He knows it's God.

And Job doesn't just bring an argument against God, though that is part of it, he seeks God, he desperately wants to hear from God, he wants to be as close to God as he was before. Job is thirsting after God.

If the Psalms had been written Job would quote: "My soul faints with longing for your salvation, but I have put my hope in your word." Psalm 119:81

It's hot out here, I want, no I need a drink of water- my soul thirsts for you oh Lord. Job wants nothing but God! In a dry and thirsty land Job wants to see God's power and His glory.

Back to Psalm 63. Hebrew texts say that David wrote this Psalm while hiding in the wilderness of Judah, maybe while on the run from Saul. Something interesting to see: what had Job done wrong to deserve being drug into the pit of despair? Absolutely nothing.

What had David done wrong that Saul sought so diligently to kill him? Absolutely nothing. You see that sometimes suffering isn't caused by anything that we have done or not done- sometimes suffering is just because this is a broken world and we are broken people. Sometimes suffering is the result of a cosmic bet between God and Satan.

Now I want us to think about something about these two people, David and Job. Would you say that they were both very mature in their relationship with God? They are not new believers are they? They have grown closer and closer to God over the years.

God calls David a man after His own heart; God calls Job a blameless and upright man. That's God speaking here!

I have a friend who is always encouraging us to grow in our faith- not be satisfied with where we are in life but to know God better and better, more and more, like Job and David, eh? Makes me wonder: what does God say about me? What does He say about you? After His own heart? Blameless and upright? Why not?

John Eldredge said in one of devotionals this week: Compare the shriveled (up) life held up as a model of Christian maturity with the life revealed in the book of Psalms:

You have made known to me the path of life; you will fill me with joy in your presence, with eternal pleasures at your right hand. (16:11)

As the deer pants for streams of water, so my soul pants for you, O God. My soul thirsts for God, for the living God. When can I go and meet with God? (42:1-2)

O God, you are my God, earnestly I seek you;

My soul thirsts for you, my body longs for you,

in a dry and weary land, where there is no water. (63:1)

Ask yourself, *could this person be promoted to a position of leadership in my church?* Heavens, no. He is far too unstable, to passionate, too desirous. It's all about pleasure and desire and thirst.

Christianity, no make that real Christianity has nothing to say to the person who is completely happy with the way things are.

God's message is for those who hunger and thirst—for those who desire life as it was meant to be. Why does Jesus appeal to desire? Because it is essential to his goal: bringing us life. He heals the crippled fellow at the pool of Bethesda. Two blind men get their sight, and the woman at the well finds the love she has been seeking.

Reflecting on these events, the apostle John looked back at what Jesus offered and what he delivered and said: "He who has the Son has life" (1 John 5:12). Life, real life, that's what I'm thirsty for!

"The glory of God is man fully alive." - St. Irenaeus

"All men die; few men ever really live." -William Wallace

Ok, now back to Psalm 63, verse 1

David is a man fully alive, really alive, mature in his faith: God you are my God. I will seek, my soul thirsts, my flesh longs.

Verse 2: I have looked for You ...

Verse 3: here's why: better than life itself. It is life itself!

I praise you, leading into verse 4: Oh no, there's the lifting up of hands again! David really is unstable, passionate, hungry and thirsty after God, lifting up his hands even!

And verse 5: Satisfied with God ... and his mouth and lips are praising God again. Ever met any silent Christians? They love to quote St Francis of Assisi: "Preach the Gospel and, if necessary, use words."

You know what? That's not true, folks we've been lied to for the last I don't know how many years. Not only did St Francis of Assis not say that, it's a cop out! What do you mean if necessary, use words? Look at David's example; it's always necessary to use words! If your mouth is not moving then you are not sharing the Gospel.

Especially in this crazy relativistic, situational ethics society we live in. How in the world will they know it's Jesus if you don't say so?

And if you do some simple research, here is what some scholars actually think that St. Francis of Assisi actually said, "Preach the Gospel Always. And for the Love of God, Use Words."

I pretty sure that's the same thing that David is saying here, my lips shall praise, my hands are lifted up, my mouth shall praise You with joyful lips ...

Seriously folks, for the love of God, use words! Say so, that's the sign of a growing Christian, a mature Christian full of faith.

Verse 6: what are you thinking about when you aren't thinking about anything- is it God? For David it is. Another sign of a mature Christian, thinking about God, continually in prayer.

Verse 7: because, therefore.

And finally verse 8: what a beautiful word picture. My soul follows close ... Your right hand holds me up.

Ask yourself:

As the deer pants for streams of water, so my soul pants for you, O God. My soul thirsts for God, for the living God. When can I go and meet with God? (42:1–2)

O God, you are my God, earnestly I seek you;
My soul thirsts for you, my body longs for you,
in a dry and weary land, where there is no water. (63:1)

Is this you? Can you say along David and we'll see later along with Job that your soul pants for God, thirsts for God, for the Living God? Does your soul thirst, does your body long for God? Do we desire God so much that we are thinking about Him always, continually in prayer?

Are we so fanatical for God that our hands lift up to our Daddy, and our lips can't help but praise Him?

Thirst for the Lord, long for the Lord, let your lips and your mouth praise the Lord. No matter what the circumstance; like David in the wilderness and Job in the depths of despair.

# IN A DRY AND THIRSTY LAND ...

*Psalm 63:1*

*Job 42:1-6*

'God works in mysterious ways, His wonders to perform,' how many times do we quote that verse when things don't go the way we were expecting? And how often do we feel that way when things happen that we don't expect?

I think that sometimes we base a lot of faith on that saying and on Romans 8:28: All things work together for good ... Perhaps that's how our finite minds try to explain the unexplainable?

Now I hate to disappoint you but that is not a Bible verse, 'God works in mysterious ways ... ' A fellow named William Cowper wrote a hymn in the 19th century that says, "God moves in a mysterious ways; His wonders to perform; He plans His footsteps in the sea, and rides upon the storm." It's a nice saying but not necessarily true and certainly not biblical.

And Romans 8:28, "And we know that all things work together for good to those who love God, to those who are the called according to *His* purpose. For whom He foreknew, He also predestined *to be* conformed to the image of His Son, that He might be the firstborn among many brethren. Moreover whom He predestined, these He also called; whom He called, these He also justified; and whom He justified, these He also glorified."

This may be more of a statement about the future, our future glorification conformed to the image of Jesus, the firstborn from the dead.

Do you think Job felt that God works in mysterious ways? And that all things work together for good? I don't think so. That is not what I read in the Book of Job. And God's final answer to Job is about sheep and goats, wind, snow, and rain, and leviathan and behemoth, to which we scratch our heads and say, huh?

I think the book of Job is more about God than it is about Job. We can see that he alone is God, he alone can lay the foundations of the earth, bring the snow, control leviathan. He is God, no matter what happens to us.

And we know that all things work together for good? Not necessarily on this earth. But someday, someday we will be glorified as was Christ.

Sometimes suffering in this life makes no sense and never will, I don't think that Job truly ever understood it. Sometimes suffering in this life can only be relieved, and even that is not a good word, sometimes suffering in this life is designed to get us to cry out to God all the more! It's designed to help us understand that God is God and we are not.

Job 42:1-6, he gets it! You are God, too wonderful for me to know.

My job in the middle of all this is twofold:

1. Job 15:13, Though He slay me, yet will I trust in Him ... that's faith!
2. I think that David says it best in so many of the Psalms. 4.1 Hear me when I call; 12.1 Help, Lord; 17.1 Attend to my cry; 22.1 My God, my God, why have you forsaken me?; 43.1 Vindicate me, O God; 69.1 Save me O God! You get the picture: Cry out to God, let him know that you know that he is God.

Will that bring relief in times of suffering? No. But I guarantee that we really do know that all things work together for good and that we will be glorified as Christ was, someday, someday.

Now, funny things always happen in life as we walk with the Holy Spirit. We learn things for a purpose, don't we? Look at Psalm 63, verse 1:
O God, You *are* my God;
Early will I seek You;
My soul thirsts for You;
My flesh longs for You
In a dry and thirsty land
Where there is no water.

Boy, have I had to deal with that thirst this week. I've been drier than the pea plants after the third picking and no rain for three weeks. I've been in that dry and thirsty land where there is no water. I wish that I could explain why- I know what Job's friends would say, I know what most of us would say: I must have done something wrong. (What did Job do wrong? What did David do wrong when he wrote Psalm 63? Oh, nothing, that's right. Why oh, why do we think so erroneously?)

There's another saying that Christians like to throw out to each other, maybe we're trying to help, maybe some are just mean spirited, I don't know. But it goes something like this: When God feels far away, guess who moved? You know, I don't find that very helpful. I know the sovereignty of God, the immutability of God, but did Job move? Did David move? Did Jesus move when He cried out from the cross, my God, why have you forsaken me?

Do you know how many times Job cries out to God with no answer? How about David here in Psalm 63? See, there is the mistake we make with our friends- we speak of things we do not know. Maybe God feels far away this week because He is far away this week, maybe I didn't do anything wrong or move anywhere.

But here is how I'm going to handle it:

Though He slay me, yet will I trust in Him.

Cry out to Him, plead with Him, thirst for Him, hunger for Him.

God really is all that there is- will I be restored? Will justice prevail? Does it matter? Yet will I trust in Him.

Do you want to know how to really, really help each other in the dry times? Do you really want to know what to say to hurting friends? Look way back in Job chapter 2:

Now when Job's three friends heard of all this adversity that had come upon him, each one came from his own place—Eliphaz the Temanite, Bildad the Shuhite, and Zophar the Naamathite. For they had made an appointment together to come and mourn with him, and to comfort him. And when they raised their eyes from afar, and did not recognize him, they lifted their voices and wept; and each one tore his robe and sprinkled dust on his head toward heaven. So they sat down with him on the ground seven days and seven nights, and no one spoke a word to him, for they saw that *his* grief was very great.

It's when they start talking that they ruin it. In chapter 19 Job asks his friends: "How long will you torment my soul,
And break me in pieces with words?
These ten times you have reproached me;
You are not ashamed *that* you have wronged me."

Sometimes the best thing to say is nothing.
There was a four year old child whose next door neighbor was an elderly gentleman who had recently lost his wife.
Upon seeing the man cry, the little boy went into the old gentleman's yard, climbed onto his lap, and just sat there.
When his Mother asked what he had said to the neighbor, the little boy said,
"Nothing, I just helped him cry."

Ten times Job's friends made him feel worse and they still have 12 chapters to go! Just help him cry! Bring a pizza and help them cry. Just be quiet-sometimes that's the best thing to do.

In several places Job pleads for an advocate, someone to plead for him to God, someone to plead his case before God. And in chapter 19:25 he knows that his Redeemer lives. This is prophecy of our Lord Jesus Christ.

You see God has things under control in the midst of unexplained suffering, in the midst of a dry and thirsty land, Jesus will come and plead our case, take our punishment for sin; I know that my Redeemer lives, He is the firstborn from the dead we saw in Romans 8 and someday, someday, all things will work together for good I will be conformed into His image, I will be like Him and all of this suffering will be over forever.

But in the meantime, encourage each other without condemnation because sometimes we really don't know why troubles come. Stay faithful, what else is there? And cry out to God, he really does want to hear from us, to be sought after, to be loved with all of our hearts and souls and minds ...

Though He slay me, yet will I trust in Him ... let that verse sink in this week. That really requires some faith.

And remember to encourage each other because we really don't understand the why's of life. But someday we will!

# WHAT'S WITH ALL THE WATER?

*Genesis 1:1-10*

It has been very dry in our state this summer. Up north they have had plenty of rain this year, the Great Lakes are at super high levels, the fern is still green this summer when normally it has turned brown by now.

It seems to me that we put a lot of emphasis on one thing when it is sorely lacking: water. Did you ever notice that? In this agricultural society we seem to be overly concerned with water. Many years ago in the newspaper business we gave away rain gauges as a promotional gift. Guess when they were most popular? During the years of drought.

Not too long ago I was in a conversation about evolution and wondered this: we hear a lot of talk about different animals evolving from such and such but you know what secularists rarely talk about? How did water come to be? It's not alive; how did it evolve or whatever you call it?

Sitting on the shore of Lake Huron you can't help but notice a lot of water. You know that lake is over 300 miles long? And it's not as big as Lake Superior! The Great Lakes hold a whole lot of water!

Funny thing too, I was reading some historical fiction about the Samaritan woman at the well from John chapter 4. Do you know that God puts a lot of emphasis on water? It's funny to hear pastors say things like, the Bible teaches more about money than even Heaven or hell, like somehow that makes a sermon on money more important?

Well I'll tell you what; the Bible talks more about water than Heaven, hell, or money. Does that mean we should have more sermons on water? I don't think that I have ever heard a sermon on water.

Well, God does have a lot to say about water starting at the very beginning, Genesis 1. Right away we see the Spirit hovering over the waters, must have been one of the first things created, eh?

I answered a question in Sunday School one time that I later regretted saying when the teacher asked, what was the Spirit of God doing hovering over the waters. Contemplating, I said, what does a butterfly look like, how will I design a raccoon, how many toes will a sloth have? You would have thought that I said the most blasphemous thing ever uttered! How dare you suggest that God needs to contemplate anything? He is God! Well, you can decide for yourself but I still like my answer.

Back to water, I always call it the elixir of life for with it we make coffee. No seriously, we have water right at the beginning, then again in chapter 2 God explains that four rivers water the Garden of Eden- that detail must be important as it is in the Bible!

But something happens and the wickedness of man was great in the earth, Genesis 6.6 says 'and every intent of the thoughts of his heart was evil continually.' Sounds like about where we are today.

And what does God use to bring judgment upon such wickedness? Of course we know, water. The Flood. And now we have God's promise to never flood the earth again, Genesis chapter 9.

But God is not done using water as an example, He is just getting started: remember Lot moving away from Abraham toward Sodom because it was a well-watered plain? Then we have Hagar kicked out of Abraham's house twice, both times finding a well right before she dies of thirst and both times receives a promise from God. How does Rebekah come to be Isaac's wife? She waters the servant's camels!

Jacob becomes known as a well digger, some of his wells still exist today. And when his family moves to Egypt with Joseph, they settle in Goshen, the flood plain of the Nile River. And we know the story of Moses drawn from the Nile and raised as a Prince of Egypt. How did he meet his wife and in-laws? At a well in Midian where he helped water their flocks.

Oh yeah, remember that thing where the Hebrews had to cross the Red Sea to escape the Egyptians?

There are many references to water as the children of Israel wonder in the desert for 40 years and remember that it was an incident with water, Moses struck the rock rather than speaking to it that kept him out of the Promised Land.

Joshua takes over and crosses the Jordan River much like the Red Sea forty years earlier and enters the Promised Land. Deborah the judge is given victory over Sisera when a deluge causes his chariots to get stuck in the mud. David wants a drink from the well in Bethlehem and three men risk their lives and travel all night behind enemy lines to get it for him.

Then we have the drought during the time of Elijah and its end with the dramatic test on Mt. Carmel- he pours a lot of water on the sacrifice just to make a point. And by the time he runs down the mountain to Samaria, it's pouring down rain!

Wow, we've seen a lot of water and we're not even one-third of the way through the Old Testament. We're not even to the Psalms yet, like a tree beside the waters, beside the still waters, poured out like water ... you understand.

On to the New Testament, we have John Baptizing in water of course. Jesus turning water into some good hooch, I mean fine wine, sounds more religious I guess, Jesus walking on the water, telling how important it is to give a cup of cold water to a child!

We haven't even looked at prophecy yet, Zechariah 9 the Lord's dominion will be from sea to sea, Zechariah 14, living water will flow from Jerusalem, one-half to the east, one-half to the west. Revelation 7, the shepherd will lead them to living fountains of water, Revelation 22 a pure river of water of life from the throne of God and on and on ...

With all that in mind, I've been thinking most about this living water, and the best example of it in John chapter 4- take a minute and turn there in your Bible. You can study this chapter again on your own but we want to look at some key points.

Verses 1-6 set the place, verse 7 the woman meets Jesus- 'give me a drink,' he says. Verse 8 is interesting as the Jews have no dealings with Samaritans unless they are hungry I guess.

Verses 9-10 here we see the living water mentioned.

Verses 11-12 her arguments. Are you greater than Jacob the well-digger?

13-14 never thirst, that water will become in him a fountain up to everlasting life!

She doesn't quite get it yet in verse 15 but she will by verse 26.

But let's look at verse 14 – 'the water becomes in him a fountain ...'

The water is within him, spiritual not physical, and when satisfied spiritually, a man will never thirst again. Jesus said to Nicodemus, "... unless one is born of water and the Spirit, he cannot enter the kingdom of God." John 3.5

And now He tells this woman at the well that she will never thirst again when filled with the Holy Spirit. Isn't that what we want? Isn't that what we need most of all? To be filled with the Holy Spirit to the point of never, never thirsting again because nothing in this dry and thirsty land can satisfy us anyway.

Two things to remember: we need Jesus, to satisfy, to quench our thirst our thirst for eternity, and if we are not filled with the Spirit, we've got nothing. Don't go another day without that life giving water that Jesus offers, washing away our sins forever!

And remember this: I hope that you never get a drink of water without thinking of it in a new and special way. I hope that it always reminds you of our Lord.

What are you thinking about when not thinking about anything? Here is how to think more and more about God, even when getting a drink of water, or giving one in Jesus's name.

# THE WEAPONS OF WARFARE

II *Corinthians 10:1-10*

My wife Teresa and I spent a week with some friends in San Diego. They seem to love it out there in southern California- it doesn't suit me much. I do love laying on the beach and the ocean breeze is cool every day, about 74 at the water, but much hotter inland, about 85 every day, and really hot in the dessert, about 105.

And here is the thing that turns me off the most: they have not had one drop of rain for over four months. You talk about a dry and thirsty land ... no grass or vegetation is still living, many of the avocado trees have died- watch for a guacamole famine in the near future. Better stock up.

Only one small brush fire of 30 acres or so trapped us in for an evening. But they take even a small fire very seriously: three helicopters, a DC-10 airplane and another smaller firefighting airplane were on the scene in minutes. They had it under control and the highway was open again in the morning. With no rain for four months you can imagine how quick a fire can spread. Makes me appreciate water more and more!

The cost of living is quite high too: their water bill averages $800 per month, utilities are around $800 per month and taxes are a whopping $1,000 per month. Don't forget the homeowners association fees to care for the private roads and driveways.

Really we were just too busy last week going here and there trying out this restaurant and that restaurant. I was so happy to eat a home cooked meal this week. I had intended to lay by the pool and read all week but I didn't get that done.

And I had intended to work on a great Bible lesson but I didn't get that done either. Every time I tried to work on something I got distracted, isn't that the way it works? But when I was up early in the morning sitting outside drinking coffee I found myself reading II Corinthians 10 again and again. I tried to study an online commentary one day without success.

I don't know if this is all relevant to what we struggle with but there must be something there-

So, look at II Corinthians 10, verse 1: Paul says that he is pleading with the church at Corinth, some versions use exhort or beseech- I'm begging you says Paul to pay attention here.

By the meekness and gentleness of Christ, I wondered how Paul can use those adjectives to describe Jesus. Jesus wasn't meek and gentle, He was a little rough and tumble we might say especially driving the vendors out of the Temple.

But here is the key: Jesus is meek and gentle and humble in this fact- he never forces Himself on anyone. It's up to you accept the free gift of Salvation, Jesus isn't going to make you. In fact, he isn't going to make you doing anything ... he is looking for a changed heart.

Paul is the same, he cannot make the Corinthians do anything, but he is pleading, begging them to pay attention. He notes that it's easier to write them a bold letter than to have a confrontation in their presence. Interesting.

Matthew Henry says this about verse 2: 'He is desirous that no occasion may be given to use severity. *He beseeches them* to give no occasion for him to be bold, or to exercise his authority against them in general, as he had resolved to do against some who unjustly charged him as *walking according to the flesh* ... '

Don't give me a reason, Paul begs, to use the authority I've been given against you as I plan to do against some that unjustly accused me of being worldly, walking according to the flesh. It seems silly to us looking back at it that somebody would accuse the Apostle Paul of being worldly doesn't it?

You think that doesn't still happen today? I'll tell you frankly that pastors and missionaries are accused of being worldly all the time. And some deservedly so! But test the spirits said Paul and John to see if it is from God. And if your accusation is not from God, then keep your mouth shut!

Verse 3: for though we walk in the flesh, we're not fighting the flesh. We can't help but be in the flesh in this world now can we? But that is not where the battle is- we wrestle not against flesh and blood but spiritual wickedness ... Paul told the Ephesians.

This isn't a physical battle, let's not try to fight it as such. Back to what I said earlier, I intended to work on a sermon sitting by the pool, I tried to read a commentary on II Corinthians 10, nothing was working!

And what's your first thought when I share those struggles? Well, he doesn't have much self-discipline now does he? Maybe he ought to quit vacationing and read his Bible and pray more. And those thoughts are exactly what Paul is talking about- accused of being in a fleshly, worldly battle. Simply put- that's wrong.

I don't need more self-discipline, I need more Jesus! We do not war according to the flesh! Do you think Paul is being truthful here?

Verse 4: if the battle is not fleshly, worldly, carnal, then the weapons aren't either. No earthly weapon can fight a spiritual battle, they just aren't strong enough.

But, there's our favorite word, our weapons are mighty in God. Aren't you glad for that? I don't have to fight this battle in my flesh, my weapons are mighty in God!

We really need to look at the entire sentence here to get the whole idea: for pulling down strongholds, casting down arguments and every high thing ...

If you are like me you have heard many sermons over the years about pulling down strongholds that Satan builds in our lives. Great, don't let Satan get a foothold to build any stronghold in our lives but it's much, much deeper than that.

I like the way the King James Version puts it: (For the weapons of our warfare are not carnal, but mighty through God to the pulling down of strong holds;) Casting down imaginations, and every high thing that exalteth itself against the knowledge of God.

Pulling down strongholds and casting down imaginations, speculations, arguments say different translations. What are these?

Simply put, these are the negative thoughts, speculations, arguments and imaginations that Satan plants in our thought process. Because when Satan plants that negative idea and we accept it, it becomes a stronghold.

I like to read books that John Eldredge writes, he is the author of that great book, *Wild at Heart*- helping men be men. John calls these speculations and arguments that turn into strongholds, 'agreements.' It works like this – back to a pastor being criticized for being worldly or in the flesh like Paul was. Paul knows that no matter who his accuser was, this is a spiritual battle. He can either agree with the accusation or he can fight it.

If he, or I or anyone one of us were to agree with Satan I might tell myself, yeah, who do I think I'm fooling- I'm just worldly in the flesh just like my critics say.

I have just agreed with evil. And if I believe it long enough, it becomes a Satanic stronghold! Now how effective will my ministry be if I myself believe I'm a phony?

Verse 5- cancel agreements with Satan, cast down those imaginations and every lofty thing raised up against the knowledge of God, bringing every thought captive to the obedience of Christ.

No matter what is said about me here in the flesh, what does Jesus Christ think about me?

This is not a fleshly battle, this is a spiritual battle. Oh sure, Satan uses people to do his dirty work, to criticize, to discourage, to gossip, to say the meanest things possible to steal our joy. But pity the person who allows themselves to be a tool of the devil!

Verse 6: we are ready to punish disobedience said Paul when your obedience is complete. Paul has the authority to punish disobedience- he would commend those whose obedience was complete and admonish those being used by Satan. And so do we.

So what should we do differently? #1 Don't allow ourselves to be used by Satan to steal joy, cause division, or spread gossip. #2 recognize that this is spiritual warfare, pity and pray for the person who gives in to evil. #3 Recognize the beginnings of strongholds from criticisms, and cast down those imaginations.

When spiritual battles come, take those thoughts captive to the obedience of Christ. It's the only way win this war.

# THE GOODNESS OF GOD

*Mark 10:17-22*

For God is Love
*I John 4:7-10*

Remember the song *God is Good (all the time)*? The Gaither Vocal Band made it famous over the years

That made me think about the goodness of God so I looked up all the Scriptures that say God is good- you can try that at home and see if you are surprised at what you find.

And after visiting southern California I think that you find a lot of people living in wealth that would agree with the Gaither's- God is good, all the time. I need to mention here that we found some good solid Christian people in southern California. I was surprised- you think of the whole state being a bunch of nuts but we attended an Evangelical Free Church and they were very, very evangelical. They were a very big church too!

But back to my point, all of the folks who drive the BMW's and Mercedes that filled the parking lot of the church would agree that yes, God is good. All the folks who live in million dollar plus houses with maids, gardeners, and a 'pool man' who comes every Wednesday to do something to the pool- they would agree that yes, yes, God is good, all the time.

And then I came across this article about the goodness of God:

"Only God is completely good in His nature and actions. His goodness includes all the positive moral attributes, such as grace, patience, and kindness.

**Illustration:** When the rich young ruler called Jesus "Good Master," Jesus reminded him that only God could be properly referred to as "good." The good that exists in the world around us truly reflects or expresses the goodness of God. There is no other source of true "good." When God revealed His name to Moses, He described Himself as being "abundant in goodness" (Exodus 34:6).

**Application:** The goodness of God is illustrated daily in our lives by the many good things that add comfort and enjoyment (James 1:17). Christians should be careful not to take these gifts for granted. Share how God has been good to you recently."

Did you catch that next to last sentence? "The goodness of God is illustrated daily in our lives by the many good things that add comfort and enjoyment."

Back to southern California for a minute: another thing I notice is that San Diego is such a city of contrasts. I have never seen so many homeless people living in public- behind every building along the railroad tracks, in tent cities on every highway walkway, under every overpass. Homeless people everywhere.

I wonder if they buy into this God is good idea? They don't seem to have many good things that add enjoyment and comfort to their daily lives. We walked away from the waterfront one afternoon and some fellow was digging in the trash can there. I wonder what he would think if I told him that God is good, all the time?

We looked at the life of Job a few chapters ago; I wonder if Job thought that God is good, all the time when he learned that his children had just been killed? Isn't that what his friends tried to tell Job? God is good, all the time - so you must have done something wrong. Hmmm, if I remember right, they were wrong as could be and God was not pleased with them at all.

It makes for a hit song by the Gaithers, it's easy for folks to say to say when they drive $100,000 cars and live in $1 million houses. It's easy for us who drive cars at all and live in houses period, and never miss a meal: God is good, all the time, but #1 I think that is too shallow of an understanding of God, and #2 it's nowhere in Scripture. Try it for yourself, search the Scriptures and see.

A deeper understanding of God can be seen in Scripture in I John, in Chapter 4 starting at verse 7: Beloved, let us love one another, for love is of God; and everyone who loves is born of God and knows God.

Let that verse sink in for a minute. Love one another, for love is from God. the proof of salvation? Everyone who loves is born of God and knows God!

Here it is, the surety of Salvation, and eternal life; everyone who loves is born of and knows God.

And verse 8 sums it all up: the one who does not love does not know God. Do we really need to make it any clearer? Sometimes the deepest understandings are the simplest. Don't love? Don't know God, it's really is that simple.

And the greatest words ever written follow: For God is love. God is love, if you don't love, you can't possibly know God. Let that sink for a minute.

Ask yourself this: do I really love, do I really love people? If you asked all the folks in your circle of friends if they thought you loved people what answer would you get? Do you really want to know? Try it!

Goodness sakes we can fool ourselves so much and we can fool other people for a while but eventually we are known by our ... what did Jesus say? Known by our love!

Verse 9- the love of God is manifested in us! In us!

And verse 10- not that we loved God, don't be silly, we really didn't before our salvation now did we? But He loved us, because God is love!

I think you maybe get my point now: God is good, all the time? Sure, I guess so, but good is so relative. The fellow digging in the trash in San Diego, say he finds one-half of a cheeseburger. Is that a good gift from God?

Would Job say that God is good? In fact we know what Job said:

'Then said his wife unto him, Dost thou still retain thine integrity? curse God, and die.

But he said unto her, Thou speakest as one of the foolish women speaketh. What? shall we receive good at the hand of God, and shall we not receive evil? In all this did not Job sin with his lips.' Job 2:9-10 KJV

Wow! Those lyrics would not sell nearly as many records would they?

It's so much better it's so much deeper, yet so much more understandable to say with the Apostle John: God is love. Think if the Gaither's had sung their song that way: God is love, yes he is, he's love all the time. God is love, you know he is, he's love all the time!

See no matter what happens in this broken world, God is still love and still loves us. "I have loved you with an everlasting love" God told His people in Jeremiah 31:3. What can separate us from the love of Christ? Paul asked in Romans 8- nothing!

God is love, and what can separate us from God? Nothing, once we are his.

God is good? Is he? I know one thing for sure: God is God, and I am not. And God is love, yes He is, all the time.

You are now, you always have been, and you will forever be loved. It might help to say that to yourself, every day. Maybe every hour. This is the boat that carries your heart right across that ocean of pain to the safe haven of God.

I am loved. Deeply and truly loved. "I have loved you with an everlasting love" God says

"What can separate us from the love of Christ?" Paul asked. Absolutely nothing.

# PROPHETS, RIGHTEOUS MEN AND DISCIPLES

*Matthew 10:40-42*

I been thinking about how each of is called to be a missionary. Oh I know that God doesn't call all of us to mysterious locations around the world like Togo; sometimes He calls us to more exotic places like St. Paris, Ohio.

The point is, and I think you will see it in the verses you read in Matthew 10 that God calls everyone one of us somewhere. You can look at this whole chapter on your own but this is what you will find: Jesus is not talking to people with any exotic calling; He is not talking to people with any specialized training, not doctors and nurses. Jesus is talking to you, to me to all of us who know Him and love Him and have assurance of forgiveness of sins and born-again salvation!

If you are part of the Church, with a capital C, then he is talking to you!

Now you might say, wait a minute, it clearly says that Jesus called the twelve disciples and that is specifically who he is talking to here in Matthew chapter ten. Ok, did the twelve have any special training? If I remember right they were fishermen, tax collectors, one was a mercenary, and one was a cheat. I don't see any doctors, lawyers, captains of industry here- none of these guys were CEO's of fortune 500 companies.

These are regular people who just happen to believe what Jesus is saying. And their specialized training? Well it's all right here in Matthew chapter

10, we can read the same thing and get the same instructions from Jesus that they did.

These verses and the whole chapter really doesn't need much explanation- you will understand it clearly when you read it. The only difference is that the twelve disciples were told to only go to the Jews, we are sent to the Gentiles cause that's what we are and where we are.

Some things to look at and understand here in verse 40:

Receive you, receive Jesus it's that simple. Don't forget that it works the other way around too- but remember, no matter how bad our society gets, no matter who far away from God we move as a nation, there always will be some who do receive you, who do receive Jesus.

Verse 41 Jesus explains what He means. Now wait just a minute, you may think, I'm no prophet. Well, in English we think of the word prophet meaning someone to whom God has given knowledge of the future, but the word means so much more than that. It means one who proclaims God, proclaims God's word.

Friends, we better be proclaiming God's word, because we have been given knowledge of the future. And besides that it doesn't take any special revelation from God to see the direction in which our world is headed.

A righteous man? Maybe you feel better with that title but the concept is the same.

And verse 42: the word disciple, literally means a learner, a student. If that's not you, then what are you doing right now? Are you reading this and studying Scripture to learn more and more about Jesus? To worship Him, to know Him better and better? To be a disciple of Jesus?

If you're not learning and growing, you're dying. There is no neutral.

See, we don't need to be nurse practitioners in Togo, that's not our job, we are called to a much exotic location: our home. We don't need to be treating aids patients.

I am almost positive that everyone here can give a cup of cold water to one of these little ones Jesus said. The point is, what you are called to do, do it!

Assuredly, truly, positively I say to you, said Jesus, you will not lose your reward.

# REPENT OR PERISH

*Luke 13:1-5*

The Lord is close to the brokenhearted; he rescues those whose spirits are crushed. Psalms 34:18

I had been working on a study from Matthew for the past two weeks or so and thought I had a pretty good lesson just about wrapped up. But then some things happened that keep distracting me.

Isn't that the way life works? We are going along laughing and making fun and enjoying life in this country pretty well. And then something happens- just like that life changes direction, in an instant.

I think of our neighbors, they like to eat out when they go to the doctor, Frisch's breakfast bar, and they were having a good time enjoying each other's company. Then the doctor comes in and says, the cancer has spread.

I remember my friend Brian. He had a checkup coming up in January, for his cancer. He had been feeling very good and thought that the doctor would say things look great, we can hook your plumbing back up. That wasn't the news he got-he was gone in a few months.

Earlier this week some longtime friends of ours lost their youngest son when he was hit by a car while riding his bicycle. It's scary how life changes in an instant.

I suppose it was same for these people Jesus talks about in Luke chapter 13. Some people come and give Him the news that Pilate has killed some Galilean worshippers right in the Temple, while they were offering their sacrifices. I am not sure what their motive was, trying to shock Jesus at the ruthlessness and boldness of Pilate?

Now you know that the common belief was that bad things only happened to people who deserved it. Remember Job's friends? Some friends, eh? These Galileans must have done something terrible to deserve God's judgement right then and there in the Temple during sacrifices for goodness sake.

We still seem to think that way today don't we? Maybe not to the extent that we say God is passing judgement, that wouldn't be politically correct, but we still think- hmmm, did he pull out in front of someone on his bike? Did rough living as a young man cause Brian's eventual cancer?

You know what I mean and if you look deep enough, there's no difference between that kind of thinking and Job's 'friends' and the people that brought this new to Jesus. Wow, I wonder what they did wrong to deserve such a terrible thing to happen to them?

Ah, but Jesus is always right to the point isn't He? No political correctness from him, no beating around the bush. Do you suppose he asks, that these Galileans were worse sinners than all the other Galileans because they suffered these things?

Can you hear Jesus say that? Doesn't that sound just like Him? Now do you suppose He asks ... and then answers. It translates from three simple words in Greek. Jesus answers his own question by saying, "No I speak to you." And the most interesting thing to me is that the word meaning no is used when the question is expected to be a positive answer!

They were expecting Jesus to answer yes to his own question. His question was what we call rhetorical, the answer is so obvious it doesn't need to be answered: is the Pope Catholic, does a bear ...? Well, you understand.

But Jesus once again is totally unexpected and He says, οὐχί, λέγω ὑμῖν. Not! I speak to you. I tell you no. But unless you repent you will likewise perish. He turns it around to repentance, not the Galileans repentance but the people He is talking to!

And because repetition is the key to understanding He tells another story: or those eighteen, do you think they were worse sinners? I tell you no, He says again, repent or you will perish too!

This rocks their world, this rocks our world and the way we think. You know what I think when I read this? That's not fair. That's just not fair at all. You mean that these Galileans didn't do anything wrong? Pilate is just that evil- then why was he allowed to murder them?

These eighteen guys crushed by a tower. They weren't worse sinners than the other folks in Jerusalem? Maybe they were good people, hard workers showing up to help build the tower thought to be an improvement to the city's water supply.

I bet those Galileans didn't get up that morning expecting to be murdered by Pilate. The yearly sacrifice is a happy time, but that changed in an instant.

Those 18 fellows were glad to have the work on such a meaningful project. They never dreamed that the tower would fall and kill them today. It's plainly not fair. Right- it's not fair.

It's not sin, not theirs, not their parents; remember when Jesus has to deal with that question when He heals a blind man? These disciples are slow learners.

Jesus then launches into a parable, we know this is a parable because it says so. Sometimes we read through the Bible and we think, that makes no sense, what in the world does a barren fig tree? Well, He is going to explain why our thinking that sin, our or our parents, somehow causes these tragedies.

Look on in Luke 13, verse 6: no fruit.

And verse 7: a little more information, it's been three years, there is no fruit. We should have had fruit by now. Cut it down he says, it's using up resources.

Verse 8: But wait, says the steward, give it one more chance, one more year. Let me dig around it and fertilize it.

Verse 9: If it bears fruit then, great! But if it still doesn't respond, then you can cut it down.

Do you see the picture? Do you see how it relates to life? Do you see how it relates to the news about the Galileans and the Tower falling?

It's thought that the fruitless fig tree is symbolic of the Jewish people, fruitless figs. And maybe so but after the Resurrection, all Christians are called to bear fruit.

What we see in verse 8 and 9 is that God's judgment is sure- if it doesn't bear fruit, it's getting cut down. But we also see that God's patience is great- let's give it another year. If it bears fruit, great! If not, cut it down.

I don't think that the three years are literal, that's just the time a fig tree should start bearing fruit, and the one year reprieve is not literal, that's just the time a fig tree should respond. We are not fig trees, but we better well be bearing fruit, because some day, God will judge.

And what did Jesus say was the remedy for bad things happening, even to good people? Repent! or you will all likewise perish. All will likewise perish without repentance. All.

God is patient, not willing that anyone should perish but that all will come to repentance. Repent!

We never know when it just might happen to us. And while we're here, until Jesus returns, let's be fruitful people.

There was a famous American folk singer, Pete Seeger who died just a few years ago. One my favorite Pete Seeger songs is called *Rye Whiskey* and I won't sing it for you but the last verse goes something like this:

'I eat when I'm hungry, I drink when I'm dry; if a tree don't fall on me, I'll live 'till I die. If a tree don't fall on me I'll live 'till I die.'

That may be silly but how deep is the message? If Pilate doesn't murder me in the Temple, I'll live 'till I die. If the Tower of Siloam doesn't fall on me, I'll live 'till I die.

That's what I want to do- live until I die. Whenever or however that might be.

# REVIVAL OR NOT?

*Nahum 1:2-8*

I am writing this around the anniversary of the September 11<sup>th</sup> terror attacks, Patriot Day we now call it.

There have been a lot of people talking about September 11, 2001 recently. Has it really been 15 years? That time has gone by quickly.

I was working at the newspaper in those times and I remember most of the details from that morning. My generation has never really experienced war and certainly this was the first attack on American soil that any of us has seen. The feelings of helplessness, the loss of security that we sensed even in Springfield, Ohio was something that I do not care to ever repeat.

That afternoon the newspaper did something that had not been done since WWII; we ran what is called an 'extra' or extra edition, a second edition of the newspaper of that day's paper. It's usually a distribution nightmare to line up 300 or more people to go out and deliver papers again after they have already gone back to bed or to another job.

I remember very clearly that this was so unusual. People were, I suppose that numb is the best word to describe it. It wasn't excitement, though that was part of it, there was some anger, much fear, but most of what folks were feeling was so dramatic that they couldn't feel anything- numb.

Do you remember 9-11? Remember what you felt that day? I do not remember what that following Sunday was like but I remember people flocking to churches in record numbers. I wonder if people are flocking to churches in record numbers today to remember?

What looked like a major revival in the United States didn't last did it? Even in the aftermath of 9-11. Do you remember that anthrax scare? Someone was sending anthrax virus through the mail. We don't hear much about that do we?

It was close to home for us because some of the first victims were newspaper people. All of our mail had to be quarantined in a portable trailer in the back parking lot. Every morning we sent one of the clerks in to sort it and open it. Before she went in she put on a complete environmental suit, breathing apparatus and all. And she threw the suit away every day and got a new one every morning. That lady was braver than I! Hope they paid her well.

But what happened? Within six months or so everything went 'back to normal' whatever normal was. Oh, there were some 'new normals' as we called them: TSA began patting down little old ladies before they got on airplanes, The Patriot Act allowed a later corrupt administration to spy on Americans for the first time ever, security at football games and at special landmarks became tighter than ever. We went through more metal detectors than I even knew existed. The Iraqi and Afghanistan Wars ... you get the picture.

The saddest thing was that church attendance returned to 'normal' very quickly, within a few weeks. Our country had been directly attacked for the first time since the War of 1812 or so and our people flocked to God- the only security we could find. But only for few weeks. By the end of October church attendance was down to where it had been and look at how we've taken God out of just about everything since then.

I wrote a book a few years ago about the greatest sermon ever preached. The sermon was given by Jonah and the message was so simple: 'in 40 days Nineveh will be destroyed' is the way it translates. We could probably sum it up in one word: repent!

Do you remember what happens to Nineveh? They all repent, from the king on down and God spares the city. Well, He spares Nineveh for another 150 years, anyway. That seems a little sad doesn't it? The greatest revival ever known to mankind doesn't last and 150 years later the city is reduced to rubble and the people killed or scattered. Over 120,000 of them according to Jonah.

Although when I think about our September 2001 revival lasting only a few weeks it makes Nineveh look pretty good doesn't it? At least we haven't been reduced to rubble- yet.

I am almost sure that Nineveh thought the same way that we think today. We are the strongest nation on earth, the most prosperous nation that has ever existed. There is no way in the world that another country can even threaten us.

That's what Nineveh thought, that's what they were. For a couple hundred years or so they were the richest, the biggest, the baddest, the only superpower on earth. No one can even threaten us!

How quickly things can happen, how quickly things can change. Joshua 2: 8-10 'Now Joshua the son of Nun, the servant of the Lord, died *when he was* one hundred and ten years old. And they buried him within the border of his inheritance at Timnath Heres, in the mountains of Ephraim, on the north side of Mount Gaash. When all that generation had been gathered to their fathers, another generation arose after them who did not know the Lord nor the work which He had done for Israel.'

One generation and the nation of Israel turns away from God. One generation- that makes what happened in Nineveh a miracle of sorts, that makes the United States of America a real miracle. We have seen what can happen in just a few weeks. For goodness sakes, we have seen how life can change in just a few minutes!

Well, all of this got me to thinking about the Book of Nahum. We don't read many lessons from Nahum now do we? I can't remember ever hearing a sermon from Nahum ... but here it is, right near the end of the Old Testament.

We don't know much about Nahum. He was Elkoshite, it says so right here in verse 1. Some scholars think that he was from around the Sea of Galilee and that the city of Capernaum, made famous in the New Testament, may have had the name Khfar Nahum which means the village of Nahum.

You can read the book for yourself this week, it's only 3 chapters and you will see that Nahum is prophesying about the destruction of the Assyrian Empire and their capital city of Nineveh. But, it's much more than that: in warning Nineveh, God is also warning Judah-hey Judah, if you don't get it back on track with God you will be destroyed just like Nineveh.

Maybe we ought to listen to his warning too? Are things much different here in the United States today than they were in those times? Oh I know what we think, they were uncivilized savages, killing their opponents who challenged their leaders, worshiping idols, offering their babies in sacrifices ...

Remember, just 150 years earlier in Nineveh there had been the biggest revival that maybe the world had ever seen! And seriously, is our country any different today? Challenge the Clintons and see if you don't die in a mysterious weight lifting accident, or fall in front of a train. Worshiping idols? We love money above all else! Child sacrifice? We murder unborn babies to satisfy our worship of money.

Hey Judah, you better pay attention to what is about to happen to Nineveh; Hey America, maybe we ought to pay attention to what happened to both of those countries!

Those six simple verses that we read in Nahum is a perfect picture of God:

God is jealous, He takes vengeance on His adversaries, He reserves wrath for His enemies.

But He is slow to anger, He is patient! He desires that no one, no one should perish, but that all come to repentance!

Sometimes we as people are funny in our thinking- we think much more of our capabilities than actually exist. We think we are math geniuses and computer geniuses when as a country we're really about number 27 in the world in our capabilities.

I saw a fellow wearing a t-shirt not too long ago that said in fancy text, "Bring it on" Now I don't know what he thought about his physical abilities but I know this much: verse 6, Who can stand before His (the Lord's) indignation (His outrage)? Who can endure the fierceness of His wrath (His anger)? Let's not overestimate our capabilities before the Lord; we simply have none.

When God finally brings judgement, it will be like Nineveh. No one will have any power against him at all. Bring it on? Hardly, that's the view of ignorance and foolishness.

Then we have verse 7: the Lord is good, He knows His people.
He provides a stronghold for His people in that day of trouble. You can count on it.

I am not making any predictions or setting any date for judgement to fall upon the United States. Who knows, maybe we will have a revival that lasts another 150 years? Who knows, judgement may fall upon us this afternoon. And that is the point- we don't know when.

Who can stand before His outrage, who can endure His anger? His fury is poured out like fire ... but the Lord is good, a stronghold, and He knows who trusts in Him. It's not a matter of whether God is on the side of the United States, it's a matter if each one of us individually are one of His, a born again believer in the Lord Jesus Christ. Nothing else matters.

# SANCTIFIED RESIGNATION

I *Peter* 3:13-17

Warning: this lesson is more questions than answers.

I've been thinking a lot about life here in the United States, life in general. You've heard the saying 'stuck in a rut' before; it makes me wonder if the whole country isn't stuck in a rut.

Think about the mundane part of life, we get up, go to work or turn on Dr. Phil if we're retired, eat lunch, come home, go back to bed, get up the next morning and do it all over again. Remember the old dunkin' donuts commercial? Time to make the donuts ...

I know that structure is good. Structure is very necessary for without it we have mayhem. But how has life gone from structured to boring? How has disciplined become mundane? And better yet, what does God want or expect for our lives?

Has the Christian life become a mundane rut? I get up every morning, go through my prayer list and read the two Bible verses from the Daily Bread. I am always at church in the same pew every Sunday morning at 10:45 am. Does that lifestyle please God? Is that really what God wants from us?

My goodness, that all sounds so boring ... we go through the same routine day after day, week after week. Let me ask you something that you need to think about seriously. Is that effective? How does what we do in our

Christian rut grow the Kingdom? How are we growing spiritually from our current lifestyles? Really?

I Peter 3:15 says to be ready to give a defense, give the reason for the hope that is within you to everyone who asks, with meekness and fear, having a good conscience, that your good conduct in Christ ...

You know what I find ironic about that passage? When was the last time anybody asked you the reason for the hope that is within you? Seriously, have you ever been in grocery store and someone comes up and says, please, you have to tell me, you are so different, I can see it in your face, what is this reason for the hope that lies within you?

Even at church- does anyone ever visit and say, wow! You folks have so much hope, I have to know, why are you so different than other churches I've visited? What is the reason for the hope that you have here?

I do not think that has ever happened. Why? I think it's partly because we take the next phrase so seriously, so wrongly seriously: with meekness and fear. You see, we live our lives in such a mundane, boring way, that there is nothing worth asking about.

Verse 14 says that if you should suffer for righteousness sake; well it's hard to suffer for righteousness sake when we don't do anything for righteousness sake. We are so worried about being too, too I don't know what. Maybe too charismatic? Are we worried about being too excited that we have become boring?

Well I suppose that we don't want people thinking that we are some kind of religious nuts or some of fanatics. Doesn't it say somewhere to all things in order and with decency? God is not a God of confusion but of peace?

Yes, taken out of context the Apostle Paul does say that in his first letter to the Corinthians but what does that have to do with a little enthusiasm for goodness sake? What does that have do with what John Eldredge calls sanctified resignation? In other words, we've given up.

We are not necessarily doing things in order and decently, we're living our lives boringly ... is that a word?

Back to I Peter 3: now seriously speaking, have any of us ever suffered for our righteousness? Have any of us ever suffered from doing good? Yes, I understand that no good deed goes unpunished, we see that every day, but do you know what? So do the heathens. You don't have to be a born again believer to have no good deed go unpunished.

When did living a righteous life become so boring, so safe, so resigned? When did we come to believe that holiness was not showing any emotion, not doing anything to rock the boat, just going along with the status quo, the establishment?

Do you think Jesus was boring? When did we get this picture of meek and mild being passive? Did Jesus suffer from doing good, did he suffer for righteousness? Read on this week in I Peter 3 and you will see the answer.

Do you think that the Apostle Paul led a predictable, boring life? Listen to what Paul says in his second letter to the Corinthians:

From the Jews five times I received forty *stripes* minus one. Three times I was beaten with rods; once I was stoned; three times I was shipwrecked; a night and a day I have been in the deep; *in* journeys often, *in* perils of waters, *in* perils of robbers, *in* perils of *my own* countrymen, *in* perils of the Gentiles, *in* perils in the city, *in* perils in the wilderness, *in* perils in the sea, *in* perils among false brethren; in weariness and toil, in sleeplessness often, in hunger and thirst, in fastings often, in cold and nakedness— besides the other things, what comes upon me daily: my deep concern for all the churches.

Does that sound like suffering for righteousness? Sure does. Does that sound like a life where people would ask, what is this hope that keeps you going? Sure does.

What is different about us? When did we surrender? When did we give up? When did righteousness and a holy life become so boring?

Listen to these few verse from Psalm 8:
When I consider Your heavens, the work of Your fingers,
The moon and the stars, which You have ordained,
What is man that You are mindful of him,
And the son of man that You visit him?
For You have made him a little lower than the angels,
And You have crowned him with glory and honor.

You have crowned him, that's us, with glory and honor. Let that sink in for a minute. We hear a lot about original sin don't we but how much do we talk about original glory? You know glory came first right?

And isn't that what we recover when we are 'born again'? A new heart, a new Spirit, the Holy Spirit, does any of that sound boring? When did Christianity become a religion of going to church and Sunday School, holding potluck lunches, being nice, and sending our second hand clothes off to third world countries? All those things are wonderful but I don't think that is what gets people's attention enough to ask, what is the reason for the hope that is within you?

Can you imagine someone saying, what's the reason you have so many carry in lunches? Why are you so nice? (well if people noticed that in us it would be a great start)

You realize that this world is at war right? Do you think that maybe some of us could come in off the bench once in a while to do some battle? We are already guaranteed the victory, don't really have anything to lose now do we?

Let's sum it up: I want to show some enthusiasm in my life, no, I want to show some fanaticism that when people see me in the grocery or at the coffee shop that they are compelled to ask, wow! What is the reason for your hope? Let's be that kind of people, let's be that kind of church where visitors say, wow! These folks are different, there is something going on here that must be from God.

That's the life that builds the Kingdom, that's the life that brings glory to God. Let's live it!

# ORIGINAL GLORY

Genesis 1:31 "Then God saw everything that He had made, and indeed it was very good."

We have probably read that verse so many times in our lives that we don't even notice it anymore do we? It's not a verse that kids learn in Sunday School or Vacation Bible School. It just kind of fills in the end of the creation story, oh yeah, God saw everything it was very good and that made up day six ... so what?

Here is what it literally says from Hebrew: And he is seeing, Elohim, all of which he made and behold! Very good.

I like that a little better than New King James, behold! Very good. And not just very good, but perfect, absolutely perfect.

And notice this is a day by day list of Creation, man and woman are included here, back at verse 27, then chapter 2 gives us the detail of what happened that day. But the point is, all of Creation, man and woman included, behold! Very good, perfect.

Man and woman were created in such perfection that they didn't wear clothes, 2:25, and they were able to walk directly with God in the very presence of God. No one has done that since ...

Exodus 33:20 But He said, "You cannot see My face, for no man can see Me and live!"

Well, we all know what happened, by Chapter 3 in Genesis man and woman had fallen into sin and God proclaims a curse on all of Creation and the perfection is gone. You know, we hear a lot about Adam and Eve's original sin, probably because it so terribly effects everything around us today, but we rarely hear about Adam and Eve's original glory, their original perfection; and that came first! Original glory! Original perfection!

Let that sink in for a minute- how would it be to be in the state of original glory? We could see the face of God and live!

Now I've been thinking about this a lot the last two weeks or so- the original glory. I think that we get too focused on original sin and forget what we were really made for- perfection! Perhaps this is what we are striving for all of lives, to get back to that original state of glory? Perhaps the ten commandments and all the Law itself was designed for man to get back to the original state of glory- those were the guidelines of what perfection looks like?

I know, I've never kept any of the ten commandments, perhaps that's why I said striving ...

But there has to be more than just accepting the fact that original sin has so destroyed me that there is no hope. What about being born-again? Doesn't Salvation return me to what I was made to be?

St Irenaeus said, "The glory of God is man fully alive." Maybe you've heard me quote that before- I want to be fully alive to bring God glory!

Now you have heard me quote several of Paul's letters where he says that Salvation doesn't make sick people well, it makes dead people alive! The glory of God is man fully alive! The problem is that many of us don't want to be fully alive; we want to stay mostly dead all day, all of our lives.

Born again, think about the concept here: can you be half-saved, half-dead? We heard an evangelist at Faith Encounter last week ask the audience how many of you are born again, indwelt by the Holy Spirit and headed for Heaven? All hands went up and he said, Great! Would you tell your face that?

He could see in our faces that we were still mostly dead! All traces of the Original Glory were gone! Why? How many of us are born-again, indwelt by the Holy Spirit and headed for Heaven? Would you tell your face? The Original Glory should be there as much as the original sin, no make that more than the original sin. He who is in you is greater than he who is in the world. I John 4:4 Maybe our face doesn't believe that verse?

If you are still in Genesis turn over to chapter 4, verse 6: why are you so angry Cain? Why does your face look mostly dead? Sin wants to destroy you but you should rule over it. Jesus took our penalty for sin, isn't that at least worth a smile once in a while?

Personal story: at the retreat I attended last week I roomed with a young man whose face was mostly dead. You can pick them out instantly when you walk in the room. One of the other fellows and I were talking about how to help him, how to pray with him because anyone who is fully alive could see that this poor fellow was mostly dead.

Now in case you're thinking that I have some ego to think that I judge someone just because of how they look, I know, you can't judge a book by its cover, but look at Genesis 4:6 again. Why are you angry? And how do I know? It shows in your face, your countenance.

And this young man soon began to talk and proved what folks were thinking to be absolutely true: angry, bitter, impatient words flowed freely. I would like to tell you that God touched his heart last weekend. We all saw the struggle, but he left the retreat still mostly dead.

So what do we do, how do we tell our faces that Original Glory is more powerful than original sin and by gum, we ought to look that way. How do we become fully alive to bring glory to God?

First, know that it is possible, we can be mostly alive and see the Original Glory and show the Original Glory. In Exodus chapter 33 there is a beautiful story of God showing Moses His glory, you can read it this week.

And go on to chapter 34 where Moses' face shines with the Glory of God so much that the people are afraid of him! He has to wear a veil over his face when he meets with people. Let that sink in- I so reflect the Glory of God that my face shines and people are afraid!

Then we have the Christmas story as recorded in Luke. These shepherds are watching sheep when all of a sudden a bunch of angels show up and issue their normal greeting: fear not! They all start repeating: Glory to God in the highest ... and the shepherds go see the Messiah, born as a baby in Bethlehem. I always wondered how they found Jesus so easily, did His glory shine? Did the shepherds reflect the glory of God in their faces?

I would bet that they did; who can meet their Savior and go away grumpy? There's a good lesson for us: who can meet Jesus and go away grumpy? Would you tell your face you've met Jesus?

And then in Luke chapter 9 we have what we call the Transfiguration. Jesus takes Peter and James and John, His favorites, and goes up into a high mountain and His robe became white and glistening, Luke says.

Then two other guys show up, Moses and Elijah 'who appeared in glory'. And when they were fully awake, that's Peter and James and John, 'they saw His glory'. What do you think that their faces looked like after that?

You can't meet Jesus and come away grumpy. The glory of God is man fully alive, completely born again, the Original Glory can, no it should be reflected in our faces.

# HEAR HIS VOICE

*Luke 8:16-18*

I read a book by Mark Batterson a few weeks ago called *Grave Robber*. It is about the miracles that Jesus performs in the book of John. Pastor Mark starts his book with everyday miracles that we take for granted: the earth in its perfect orbit around the sun, birds and bees overcoming the force of gravity to fly, things that we don't even notice in the busyness of day to day life.

He points out the miracle of our senses and our bodies. Do you realize how complex your eye is? How about hearing? Do we realize what a miracle occurs every time we simply hear someone speaking? How about our thumbs- we have no idea how this thing works, the opposable digit.

And we haven't even touched on the miracle, the complexity of our brains. 100 billion neurons interconnected by trillions of synaptic nerves, doing uncountable calculations every second. And memory, just how does a three pound gelatinous mass of mostly water store memories? We have no idea, it truly is miraculous. By the way, there are only about 10 billion stars in the average galaxy and only about 10 billion galaxies in the universe. Your brain is infinitely more complex than the universe. Maybe we should act like it?

Back to hearing for a minute: vocal chords move air molecules which travel across space and make your eardrum vibrate which goes on through, well you get the point; it's complicated, a miracle of sorts.

The men's retreat I went to a few weeks ago had the theme of hearing God's voice. Funny thing though, only once in my life have I ever heard the still small voice of God, and I about wrecked my truck because I was driving. Some of the guys tease me saying that's why God hasn't spoken to me since. I might just run off the road with surprise!

Look at the verses we read in Luke again and go back to verse 4 to get the whole picture here, because I think that like miracles, we take some of these things for granted- we read them and think, I've heard that so many times before ... ha! Heard that so many times before ...

Start at verse 4 through verse 10. Do you begin to see a pattern here that you may not have noticed before? We think this parable is about the word in the different soils and the fruit it produces, but it's so, so much deeper in meaning: he who ears let him hear! Now why did Jesus end the story with that?

And verses 9-10 seeing they may not see and hearing they may not understand. And verses 11-15 Jesus explains about hearing the word of God. Hearing the word of God, that is what my retreat was all about! Hearing the word of God, let that sink in for a minute. Hearing the word of God, would you wreck the car? Would you be surprised? Do you want to hear the word of God, or are we afraid of what He might have to say?

That's not as unusual as you might think. My guess is that most of us don't want to hear the word of God, what he tells me to do is so inconvenient. I told a story last week of some fellow in Wendy's that I was compelled to go and speak to but didn't. Was I hearing God's word and able to ignore it? I'm afraid so ...

You can call it the prompting of the Holy Spirit or whatever you like but here is what it is: God's word, speaking to your heart. Go talk to that person- not now Lord I haven't finished my fries ... and I want to get a frosty to go. Besides that, that guy is so full of the original glory that he is scary!

I probably missed a blessing didn't I? He may have encouraged me! Why oh, why do I yearn to hear God's voice and then ignore it when it when it comes?

I said that maybe we don't want to hear God's word, God's voice because we are scared of what He might say. Well that's not a new concept. Back in Genesis 3:8-10 right after eating from the tree Adam and Eve have this conversation with God: And they heard the sound of the Lord God walking in the garden in the cool of the day, and Adam and his wife hid themselves from the presence of the Lord God among the trees of the garden.

Then the Lord God called to Adam and said to him, "Where *are* you?"

So he said, "I heard Your voice in the garden, and I was afraid because I was naked; and I hid myself."

Hearing God's voice became fearful at that moment and for most people it still is ... how sad is that? All of a sudden that most intimate relationship with God became fearful, I heard your voice and I was afraid ...

Right after the Ten Commandments in Exodus 20:18-19 we read this interesting exchange: Now all the people witnessed the thunderings, the lightning flashes, the sound of the trumpet, and the mountain smoking; and when the people saw *it*, they trembled and stood afar off. Then they said to Moses, "You speak with us, and we will hear; but let not God speak with us, lest we die."

Don't let God speak to us, we're scared, we haven't finished our lunch, we are afraid that He will want something out of us- which probably hits the nail right on the head these days. I am afraid that God will tell me to stop being so bitter, to watch my tongue, to be a witness to my family and my neighbors ... my goodness, I don't want to hear His voice, I might have to do something or change something!

He might call me to be a missionary to Togo or some awful place like that where they don't even have running water! No, let not God speak with us, like the Hebrew children said.

If you kept your finger in Luke 8 look at the verses we read, 16-18. Once again we take these verse for granted but look deeper into what Jesus is saying here. Your Bible may have a heading about a parable of light or 'our light not to be hidden' but there is so much more.

Verse 16 – we don't hide the light! Let folks see it!

Verse 17- I know many sermons have been preached to scare people into behaving because everything will be revealed, nothing is kept secret ... funny, nothing that Jesus has said so far in His whole conversation starting at verse 8 has anything to do with our good or bad behavior. He is talking about hearing God's voice all this time and now about our witness that comes from hearing the word.

Verse 18- here is the summation: take head how you hear, be careful how you hear. For whoever has more will be given, and whoever does not have, even what he seems to have will be taken away.

What is Jesus talking about? Stuff? That's the way we like to interpret it. We like to tie this in with the story of the servants and the talents- give the guy with ten talents, ten more- right? And take the one talent that the disobedient servant has.

But that is not what this says, Jesus mentions nothing about talents or behavior or stuff, He has been talking about hearing and shining! Whoever hears and shines, more will be given to him, more and more opportunity to hear, with a good and noble heart verse 15, and bear more and more fruit!

The more we hear and do the more and more God speaks, the more and more fruit our lives produce.

But whoever does not have, even what he thinks he has will be taken away. Even what he thinks he has ... sorry, seeing you will not see, hearing you will not understand, verse 10. You think you see, no, you think you hear, not God you don't.

Be careful how you hear, I am so afraid that if I squelch the Holy Spirit enough by being too busy eating French fries that eventually I won't get a chance to let my light shine, to bring forth fruit. He who has ears, let him hear!

Let's practice not just listening for the voice of God but hearing the voice of God. And when it comes, let's do what He asks of us, even if it's in the middle of lunch.

You know the old saying, practice makes perfect ... well that's not true. Practice makes permanent. If you practice poorly, you will play poorly, permanently.

Let's practice hearing God's voice well. As we get better and better, the more and more He will speak to us. He promises.

# ... AND THAT'S THE TRUTH.

*Matthew* 7:24-27

I had a rough week last week. On Tuesday afternoon I finally went to see the doctor for a sinus infection and got a prescription for antibiotic and Flonase to reduce the swelling and inflammation. Interesting, I had not been to the doctor for being sick since around 2000-2001. I get my regular six month checkups and blood tests but I had not been sick in over fifteen years.

It felt like I wasted a week off as I didn't feel like doing much. One day I never got off of the couch except to turn over and lay the other way. Funny how things go isn't it? I've been looking forward to fall break for months, making plans to go north camping and fishing. Then when the time comes I feel so bad that I just lay on the couch. Sounds disappointing doesn't it?

But that's not entirely true: I installed a dog door on our back porch one day; that made our I little dogs, Charlie and Barkley happy. Teresa and I picked up 500 pounds of pig feed one morning; that made the pigs happy. One of our students and I rode horses one afternoon; that made him happy but it hurt my back a little ...

Time really is never wasted is it? It goes by anyway, not wasted per se but used in different ways. Now maybe those things: a dog door, buying pig feed, horseback riding, napping on the couch, don't directly build the Kingdom- that's okay too. Maybe God knew better than I how I should spend my time last week ...

Monday evening I thought about watching football and instead I came across a channel that was showing old television shows of the late 1960's and early 1970's. Sonny and Cher came on at 8:00 pm, remember Sonny and Cher? That was before he died and she went a little, no, make that a lot of crazy.

You know that I get nostalgic sometimes so I turned on Sonny and Cher. The next show coming on was the Smothers Brothers and I was thinking that Lilly Tomlin's character, Ernestine was on that show. Remember her? She sat in a huge rocking chair and ended her spiel with "...and that's the truth, thththththt"

Well, I never made it that far. After about 2 minutes of Sonny and Cher I tired of the 1970's; yeah, they weren't that great were they? And later it dawned on me that Lilly Tomlin was on Laugh In not Smothers Brothers. I am glad I didn't stay up to be further disappointed. Now, back to my nap on the couch.

That's the truth- made me think, what is truth? That question has been asked since the dawn of time. Listen to the Gospel of John chapter 18, Jesus and Pilate:

Pilate therefore said to Him, "Are You a king then?"

Jesus answered, "You say *rightly* that I am a king. For this cause I was born, and for this cause I have come into the world, that I should bear witness to the truth. Everyone who is of the truth hears My voice."

Pilate said to Him, "What is truth?" And when he had said this, he went out again to the Jews, and said to them, "I find no fault in Him at all.

I bear witness of the truth, everyone who is of the truth hears my voice, said Jesus. Here is truth, Jesus offers Pilate. And what does Pilate do? He rejects it, he rejects the truth. Doesn't he realize that the Way, the Truth, and the Life is standing right in front of him? He sees it, but still rejects it.

Does that make you wonder at all? How can someone see the truth and yet still reject the truth? That would be a good question for our society today, for the church today. How can you so clearly see the truth and still reject it?

Which brings me to point number 1 with what we can do when confronted with truth: reject it. Just flat out reject it. This is truth, you say no it's not and go on with life.

Remember the parable of the sower in Matthew 13? We talked about it in being careful how you hear the voice of God. But a good point to look at that passage again is this: All the people represented by the different soils heard the truth. They not only heard the truth, they knew it was truth.

Look at Matthew 13:18-23 again. Now perhaps we could make an argument that the seed eaten by the birds is no rejection of the truth, as they do not understand it. But verse 20 is clear understanding, they receive it with joy. But, no root. Overall rejection. This is too hard.

Point #1, when presented with truth, it is possible to reject it.
Point #2, when presented with truth, it is possible to recreate it into your own truth.

Isn't this what happens so often in our country today? We might stick a fancy label on it and call it relativism, or call it anything you like but this is what happens so often. What is truth asked Pilate; your truth may not be my truth.

Several years ago I had the chance to meet Steven Covey, remember the books he wrote about the *Seven Habits of Highly Successful People?* Then there was the Franklin-Covey Planners, guaranteeing success for anyone who used their calendars and to-do list in their leather bound $200 planner.

I knew Steven Covey was a Mormon and he certainly appeared to be one of those highly relativistic enlightened thinkers that the world so admires. So what would you ask Steven Covey? I asked him about Jesus.

What about Jesus? See he had just written a new book about *Seven Habits of Highly Successful Families* and I asked him, how can you leave out Jesus, Salvation in Jesus? Isn't faith in Jesus the ultimate success, what else matters?

"Ah, grasshopper," he replied, (I was a much younger man then), "Jesus may be right for you and your family, but for others, they have chosen a different path of success. Jesus is just one way of the many roads to God."

I think that you're wrong Dr. Covey. I think that you just created your own truth. And now that he has passed on, I think that he does know the truth.

Go back to the verse in Matthew chapter 7, a familiar story, we used to sing a Sunday School song about it, remember? The wise man built his house upon the Rock and the rains came tumbling down ...

But start at verse 26- let's look at it in reverse because that happens more today.

Everyone who hears and doesn't do ...

Did you catch that? Especially as it relates to truth: hears, but does not do. I heard you Lord, I felt the prompting of the Holy Spirit, I know truth when I see it or hear it, but I am still going to build my life on my own foundation.

Building on the sand isn't just rejecting the truth, it's going against the truth, or like Dr. Covey developing your own truth. And when the floods come, and they will, the foundation is broken and great is the fall ...

Point #1: reject the truth
Point #2: create your own truth
Point #3: accept the truth

We know from Matthew 13 that the people who have the good ground bear fruit, lots and lots of fruit! These are the Kingdom builders. Accept the truth, accept the Way, the Truth and Life of Jesus Christ is the Savior, your Savior.

But, point #3, comes with a condition. Back to Matthew 7, verse 24-25. I know how we immediately think: wait a minute, there are no conditions to Salvation. There you go getting all liberal on us again. What about truth?

Without getting into the philosophy of the definition of truth let's just agree that God's Word is truth. Read verse 24 again: whoever hears and does. Let that sink in for a minute: whoever hears and does. It's not enough to know the truth, the demons know there is God and they tremble, faith without works is dead ... from the book of James.

Whoever hears and does, that's the condition, hear and do. Because if not, if it's hearing without doing, that's like a fool, building on the sand. And the fall of that house was great.

Let's be that kind of people, hearers and doers. The Kingdom isn't built here in this building, it's built out there, in the workplace, in the grocery store, in our families. Don't just know the truth, do the truth.

# ... AND THEN THE END WILL COME.

*Matthew 24:1-14*

I like polls and surveys even though as a former marketer I know how easily the data can be manipulated. The newspaper always used lots of polls and surveys- maybe that's how things got so messed up. In Dayton, Ohio we had our own department that did reader and advertiser surveys.

I won't go into all the details of the silliness that came out of that department but I do remember our survey director giving us a big presentation about a vast untapped market that he had discovered in Champaign County, Ohio. This area was so underserved by the media if we would just start running some stories about these cities, why circulation would probably double.

Of course he meant Quincy and DeGraff, Ohio and if circulation doubled we would have 25 readers instead of 12 ... see how data can be misconstrued? He almost convinced the executive team to restructure the editorial coverage to dedicate a certain amount of space to Quincy and DeGraff news. We would have spent $100's of thousands of dollars to reach 12 new people, maybe.

Well this week a survey came out by Lifeway Research, about 12 issues that evangelicals believe. Remember, we can make data say about whatever we want it to but even so, these numbers are very interesting.

Remember, these are people who call themselves evangelical.

1.  77% said that people must contribute their own effort for personal salvation, 52% said that good deeds help them earn a spot in Heaven.

    Guess they never hear Ephesians 2:8-9 For by grace you have been saved through faith, and that not of yourselves; *it is* the gift of God, not of works, lest anyone should boast.
2.  64% described heaven as where, "all people will ultimately be reunited with their loved ones." Basically, everyone goes to Heaven.
3.  65% said that people are good by nature, 74% said that small sins do not deserve eternal damnation. Romans 3:23 For all have sinned and fall short of the glory of God.
4.  48% said that God accepts all kinds of worship, which included Christianity, Judaism and Islam.
5.  52% agreed that Jesus is the, "first and greatest being created by God."
6.  56% said the Holy Spirit is not a person, but a force. (That explains it, right Star Wars fans?)
7.  51% said the Bible was written for each person to interpret as he or she chooses.
8.  44% said that sex outside of marriage is not a sin.
9.  The numbers are confusing in the next question but 87% said that abortion is a sin. 40% said it is not ... people just don't know.
10. 32% said that gender identity is a choice.
11. 42% said that the Bible's condemnation of homosexual behavior does not apply today. (Well, not if the Bible is to be interpreted as we want, I guess not.)
12. This one is almost funny: 37% agreed that God rewards true faith with material blessings, but only 23% of non-evangelicals agree with the prosperity Gospel. Here is even funnier: poorer and less educated evangelicals are more likely to agree with prosperity Gospel than wealthier and more schooled.

Same with lottery tickets; poorer and less educated folks are more likely to buy a lottery ticket, or support Joel Osteen, the same thing. They are buying a spiritual lottery ticket!

Look at Matthew 24, verse 4-5: many will come in My name said Jesus and deceive many.

I've always read these verses and thought: false prophets will proclaim that they are Jesus, but that would be easy to spot wouldn't it? As I look at our society I don't think that is how Satan works, they don't profess themselves to be Jesus, but they have surely come in His name to offer a way that has deceived many. They may not say that they are Jesus but they claim to know Messiah.

And many, many are deceived. What we just read!

Verse 6: wars and rumors of wars- but do not be troubled! That's easy to read but harder to do isn't it? We are concerned that our way of life will be disrupted, and I'll tell you frankly that one day, it will be.

Nation against nation, kingdom against kingdom, famine, earthquakes, pestilences, natural disasters. All these have to happen.

Verse 9: hated for Jesus' name sake.

Verse 10: many will be offended. Offended by what? When we just read through verse we think, offended by Jesus but that is not what it says. Just that many will be offended, betray one another, judged condemned or punished and hate one another. You know what I think this is? Political correctness.

Many will be offended- well we already know that you will be hated and killed for the sake of Jesus, but many, outside of Christ even, will be offended and judge one another and hate one another.

That sure looks like what is going on in our country, and in the world today. Everybody is offended about something. And they pass judgment on those who do not agree with them.

Verse 11: many false prophets, and I love this Greek word: pysdoprofaytrace, one who, acting the part of a divinely inspired prophet, utters falsehoods under the name of divine prophecies.

I guess that definition was too long to write so they just said false prophets. But think about what we saw in the survey and how it relates: falsehoods under the name of divine, they call themselves evangelicals but they utter falsehoods and the people are deceived!

Verse 12: here are some of the saddest words ever written; love will grow cold. Because of lawlessness, oh this word is so interesting too, *anomiah*. I found one dictionary where it is translated unparacleeing. Unparacleeing? What in the world is that? Well, the Holy Spirit, the one that 56% said is a force, not a person, is called a Paracleet in the New Testament, meaning one who comes along side, a helper, He stands with us. So, an unparaclete must be someone who does not come along side, does not help, does not stand with us.

Because we no longer help our neighbor, the love of many will grow cold. That's my neighborhood right now.

Verse 13: it's not all gloom! He who endures to the end will be saved! Don't give up, don't be fooled, don't be deceived like the folks in the survey. Don't be offended, that's silly. Don't listen to all these false prophets. Don't unparacleet your neighbors. But, he who endures will be saved!

Ok, one last Greek lesson, endures, *hupomeinas*, literally means stays under. Stays under what? The truth! That's what! Stay under the truth, we do not add to our salvation, God does not accept all forms of worship, everyone does not go to Heaven, the Holy Spirit is not the force, Jesus is not a created being ... stay under the truth!

One last thing to look at in verse 14: I know that we take this so literally sometimes and say that we have to get the Gospel to all people groups before Jesus can return. Well, that's not really what He is saying here.

It literally says that it must told, this good news of the Kingdom, to all nations. And then the end will come. But who does this? The good news of the kingdom must be told, by whom? I think that we already know ... I don't think that we jump in an airplane and search for an underserved unknowing people group deep in the Amazon rain forest. Goodness sake, there are plenty of people right here, in Quincy and DeGraff, Ohio, ones that call themselves evangelical even, who need to hear the good news of the kingdom, from us.

And then the end will come.

Let me ask a serious question: are you satisfied with the way our country is going? Are you happy with the way people believe according to this survey? Are you pleased with the way your church is?

If your answer is 'no' then what are you doing about it? Something to think about this week ...

# WE WIN!

*Revelation 1:1-3*

Living in this world long enough, it's pretty easy to get down in the dumps isn't it? I told my wife Teresa that I really need to hear some good news for a change ... something good needs to happen.

I know that we are in a spiritual war, and in war there are casualties. People get taken out all around us. Someday we too may finally become a casualty of war. That can be a little depressing, can't it? If we live long enough we become a casualty of war.

I guess that is why faith and perseverance are so important. Without faith it is impossible to please God, the just shall live by faith, he who overcomes will eventually eat from the tree of life. We have to keep going no matter what. *Strengthen the hands which hang down, and the feeble knees, and make straight the paths for your feet, so that what is lame may not be dislocated, but rather be healed.* Hebrews 12:12

The whole book of Hebrews is about keep going, don't give up and head back to Egypt, don't take yourself out of the battle, getting taken out will happen soon enough. Keep fighting for the promise.

Well, ok, but how do we strengthen the hands that hang down and the feeble knees? How do we find the strength to keep fighting the battle?

Well, right here is one way: we encourage each other, we've got each other's back; Sunday morning church service is a short R&R from the battlefield to keep each other encouraged.

Sometimes we need a little bit longer vacation, just to get refreshed and revived to get back in here and fight another round. That's why I like those men's retreats that I sneak off to from time to time. It's a break from the daily battle.

This week I rediscovered another way to get fired back up to get back into the battle: I simply read the end of the story. In the heat of war, bombs going off around us, bullets flying over our heads, families falling apart right before our eyes, friends dying of cancer, with all of that going on it's easy to forget that we already know how this war ends! I tend to forget, do you?

So, about the middle of last week when I needed a break from war, I went back and just read the first few chapters of The Revelation again and checked out some study notes from a class a year or so ago. In case you haven't read this book or have forgotten what it says I'll sum it up for you: Jesus wins in the end, and we win with Him!

Let that sink in for a minute- God gives us the end of the story before it even happens and we win! Awesome huh?

The Revelation of Jesus Christ we read in verse 1 of this wonderful book, which God gave to Him to show His servants. I love it! Here's how it ends folks, God might have said in modern English.

I had to write an article for publication about The Revelation when I took the class I mentioned and here is how I started it: "The *apokalupsis*, the taking the covers off of the glory of the Lord Jesus Christ and revealing Him to His servants, specifically his bondservant John, is the least taught and preached upon from the pulpit book of Scriptures. Some will go so far to say that Revelation does not belong in the cannon as did Luther, and Calvin had a unique way of dealing with the book: he ignored it."

Ignored it! I think he missed a blessing! When times get down when the battle gets so hot that it appears we could get taken out any minute, go back and read Revelation- we win in the end! What could be better to keep us going? What could be better to help those hanging hands and feeble knees?

So, start again at the beginning: verse 1. The Father gives this Revelation to Jesus and Jesus shows it to John. Remember that John was called the beloved disciple, think that Jesus liked him best?

Read verse 2: John bore witness of all the things that Jesus showed him, things that must shortly happen, real events, signs and symbols, John saw it and wrote it down.

Read verse 3: Blessed is he ... I know you've missed a blessing by ignoring The Revelation, it says so right here! Blessed is he, for the time is near. Here is the reminder of what happens in the end.

Let's go on to verses 4-6: you see that the number 7 is the number of completion in Scripture.

To help understand that there are six ministrations of the Spirit fulfilled here with Christ's rule as number 7 (my thoughts), we turn to Isaiah 11:1-2: There shall come forth a Rod from the stem of Jesse,
And a Branch shall grow out of his roots.
The Spirit of the Lord shall rest upon Him,
The Spirit of wisdom and understanding,
The Spirit of counsel and might,
The Spirit of knowledge and of the fear of the Lord.

John is revealing the past, present and future activity of Jesus: faithful witness, firstborn from the dead (He never died again), ruler of the kings of the earth.

Who loves us, present tense is a better translation, and loosed us, one time only past tense, from our sins in His blood!

And made us kings and priests- wow! How can we lose the war with Jesus leading us? To God be the glory and dominion forever amen!

Behold, John says, pay attention here. This is not an abstract, not a symbolic idea, this is real, literal. He is coming, Jesus is coming and every eye will see Him and know that He is Lord. Israel will see Him and know for sure who He is, and all the earth will mourn – because then it will be too late. How can we worry when this is our Lord and Savior?

And in verse 8 Jesus describes Himself: I Am!

In verses 9-11 John gives us the background and occasion for writing The Revelation, how Jesus gives him the information and instructs him to write it in a book. John is in exile on the Isle of Patmos where slave labor worked in the quarries during the time of persecution of Christians under the Roman Emperor Domitian.

John is 'in the Spirit', is this an out of body experience where special Revelation is given to him, does he mean Sunday when he says Lord's Day, or is John given a special vision of the Day of the Lord in the future? We are not sure, but he is told, what you see, write! And send the book to the seven churches.

In verses 12-16, John turns to see who this is speaking to him. And here is Jesus in all of His glory. John had seen the transfiguration where Jesus was briefly glorified, but now this is permanent, not Jesus meek and mild but Jesus as Lord and King.

Some symbolism needs to be explained here: the seven lampstands are seven churches, Jesus is our High Priest standing in the midst caring for His churches just as the high priest would have tended the lampstand in the Temple.

Now John describes Jesus as best he can, Jesus in all of His glory: the white hair of the Ancient of Days full of wisdom, the eyes of fire which symbolize judgment or deliverance, the feet of bronze are symbols of swift judgement, the seven starts reflecting his face and his face like the sun. The sword is two-edged for offense, striking judgment.

And John naturally falls at His feet like a dead man. He is so overwhelmed with emotion that he cannot move. Believe me, one day, every knee will bow, every tongue will confess that Jesus Christ is Lord- some to eternal damnation, some to eternal life. The choice is ours now; then it will be too late.

In verses 17-18 Jesus describes himself again: I AM, First and Last, I AM He who lives, and I AM alive forever, Amen!

I have the keys of Hell and Death, I have control over eternity!

Fear not?! Why of course, fear not! What in this world do we have to fear when our Lord and Savior is the Great I AM. Why get down in the dumps when we know who wins in the end? Jesus; every eye will see Him, every person will know that he is God!

There are two things that we need to remember: 1. don't let Satan steal our joy, even Hell and Death are controlled by Jesus. What can man do to me?

2. don't let another day go by without being sure that Jesus Christ is your Savior.

Judgment will come, those fiery eyes, those burnished bronze feet will quickly bring either condemnation or judgment. Don't be one of the tribes of the earth who weep at His coming. I want to be glad to see Him!

# DEAR CHURCH,

*The Revelation 2:1-7*

Last chapter we looked at Revelation 1:20 where Jesus explains the symbolism of the seven stars and seven lampstands: angels and churches.

The seven churches are seven literal places, real churches, real places that existed in the first century A.D. This is not symbolism.

Are these literal angels, beings who actually watch over these seven churches? Why not? We know a spiritual battle wages all around us, we get glimpses from time to time.

More important is this: Jesus is speaking, John is writing, the angel of the church is receiving, but the Holy Spirit is the One who speaks to the Church, and to us. Seven times Jesus says, "He who has ears let him hear what the Spirit says to the churches ..." seven times.

Chapters 2 and 3 of The Revelation are unique in all of Scripture- here we have the Epistles of Jesus! We know the Epistles of Paul, we know the Epistles of Peter, and now we have the Epistles of Jesus. Jesus is writing letters to the seven churches just as Paul wrote letters to the churches.

Did you ever think of that before? These 2 chapters could have been separate books, written directly by Jesus to the churches, and through the Spirit, right to us! Verse 7: "He who has ears let him hear what the Spirit says to the churches ..." Just like Paul's letters to the churches are also for us, so Jesus' letters to the churches are for us.

Look at chapter 2 for the first letter from Jesus. In verse 1, Jesus identifies Himself: I hold the stars, I tend the lampstands as High Priest forever.

Each of these letters of Jesus follows a pattern: Jesus identifies Himself, gives the church a commendation (if present), states their offense or makes accusation (if need be), and offers a warning and a promise.

So, Jesus identifies Himself, and verse 2-3 commends them: their works, their patience, they cannot bear evil, they discernment, and perseverance. They are doing it! Sounds like a busy, busy church.

Nevertheless, here comes the offense in verse 4: you left your first love. They are just doing stuff out of principle, not for people. Plenty of church programs, no love.

So sad- it reminded me of a song a buddy of mine wrote, David Fullen. My wife Teresa said I listen to the strangest music ... ok, it is a little weird, make a lot weird but it's a good weird. Besides a professional musician and music producer, Dave trains Olympic level ping pong players, sorry make that table tennis. Here is verse 3 of a song called *The Poser* (faker):

*Hello my name is Michael, I'm a poser*
*My mission is to save the hearts of men, it's right and good*
*But I don't really love them, even though I know I should*
*My motives are a mystery ...*

Oh church, God does not call us to help people, He calls us to love people. We have it so backwards. Yes doing is important, faith without works is dead as in dead, but first, the first love, the first is love! Don't make your motives a mystery church because ...

Look at verse 5: remember and repent! Yes, we need to repent of our loveless existence. Lord, help me to love people and see them as you see them, through your eyes. Forgive me for doing without loving.

And unless we repent Christ will come quickly and remove the lampstand. Matthew Henry in his commentary says this, "...he will unchurch them, take away his gospel, his ministers, and his ordinances from them ..." I am not sure what the church becomes after being unchurched, having the gospel taken away, and losing ministers and ordinances, but I do not want to find out!

And now verse 6: But, here the word but becomes a word of encouragement. But this you have, you hate the deeds of the Nicolaitans, which I also hate. We don't like that word hate do we? And we sure don't like to hear that word when used about Jesus. God is love, Jesus love me this I know ... we like the love part about God but we don't like the judgment part about God do we?

And yet, that really is what this book is all about- God's judgement. If he wins in the end, then we have to look at God wins over what? Yes, we know that we battle not against flesh and blood but there will be flesh and blood involved in the end. Lots of it.

Revelation Chapter 5 says, "...and that people should kill one another ... a fourth of the earth, to kill with sword, with hunger, with death ..." And these are just two of the seven seals of judgement!

So who are these Nicolaitans and why does Jesus hate them? (I know we could make the argument that he hates their deeds not them). Well, we are not sure; some say that Nicholas named in Acts 6 became a heretic and deceived people within the early church to follow him and some crazy doctrines about pagan rituals.

Some say there was no person but a movement within the church named Nicolaitan by the merging of two Greek words: *nico* meaning victory, and *laos* meaning people. Not victory of the people but victory over the people thus creating a division in the church which still exists today: the laity and the clergy.

Interesting isn't it? Jesus hates the doctrine of the clergy and the laity? I think that a lot of pastors would be disappointed to hear that.

And now verse 7: He who has ears better listen up to what the Spirit says. And here is great hope: overcomers get to eat from the tree of life which is in the midst of the Paradise of God. The Paradise of God, the word *paradiso* is sometimes translated Eden. That sounds restful just thinking about it...

The tree of life, clear back to the Garden of Eden in Genesis 2:8-9 we see that the Lord God planted a garden eastward in Eden, and there He put the man whom He had formed. And out of the ground the Lord God made every tree grow that is pleasant to the sight and good for food. The tree of life *was* also in the midst of the garden, and the tree of the knowledge of good and evil.

(By the way, the garden was not called Eden, the garden was in Eden, on the east side- it is always called the garden of Eden or in Eden. Remember *paradiso* in Greek is sometimes translated Eden? Adam and Eve lived in Paradise, Eden, in a garden.)

Well, we know what happened- God said that you can eat of every tree of the garden freely, but one: the tree of the knowledge of good and evil. They had one rule and couldn't keep it.

So, 'Then the Lord God said, "Behold, the man has become like one of Us, to know good and evil. And now, lest he put out his hand and take also of the tree of life, and eat, and live forever"' God drives them out of the garden and guards the entrance with a cherubim with a flaming sword. Not so they would not live Eden, they still did, not so they couldn't enjoy the garden, but so they could not eat from the tree of life and live forever- because now they are in a sinful state. Who wants to live forever in these sinful bodies?

Remember Jesus is the firstborn from the dead in the Revelation chapter 1? So will we be like Him in Paradise. And once these sinful bodies are made new, we can eat from the tree of life! Just like Adam and Eve were made to do.

He who has ears let him hear! Overcomers will be given the right to eat from the tree of life, in the midst of the Paradise of God. I wonder what it tastes like?

As a people of God, let's remember our first love: to love the Lord your God with all of your heart and strength and mind, and love our neighbors as ourselves. It really is that simple and yet that difficult.

# THANKS FOR SOMETHING

I *Thessalonians 1*

I am writing this right before Thanksgiving in mid-November.

Can it really be the week of Thanksgiving already? This year went by so fast. Only 35 days until Christmas or something like that.

We like the story of the pilgrims and the Indians coming together for the first Thanksgiving back in 1621. Remember in grade school we would even make construction paper outfits, some kids were Indians, some kids were the pilgrims. I think that I was always the turkey ...

Remember tracing your hand on a piece of paper and coloring it into a turkey? Whatever happened to those simpler times? You probably aren't allowed to do those things in school anymore, somebody, somewhere is offended. Well, you know how that goes.

It wasn't until 1789 that President George Washington made a proclamation to celebrate Thanksgiving once a year as a nation, and not until 1863 did Abraham Lincoln make it into a federal holiday to be celebrated in November.

This year I've been thinking about being thankful, I think that's the idea of the holiday, and of course my first thoughts are that there really isn't much to be thankful for right now. We seem to be going through some tough times, difficult things are happening all around us.

I was thinking about losing family members. We have a friend coming up on the one year anniversary of losing her husband- she's going through a tough time. It's been five years last week that my mother died, and four years ago yesterday that my father died.

I talked twice to an old friend this week, he is not doing well- I really thought that his first call was to say goodbye, he sounded that depressed. I talked to a family this week looking for some help for their son and I came away with the feeling that that their situation was hopeless, completely hopeless.

Satan wants us to feel that way doesn't he? I went back and read Lincoln's proclamation making Thanksgiving a federal holiday:

"The year that is drawing towards its close, has been filled with the blessings of fruitful fields and healthful skies. To these bounties, which are so constantly enjoyed that we are prone to forget the source from which they come, others have been added, which are of so extraordinary a nature, that they cannot fail to penetrate and soften even the heart which is habitually insensible to the ever watchful providence of Almighty God."

I am prone to forget the source of the bounties that we enjoy, fruitful fields, healthful skies. And when I think of the extraordinary blessings, they cannot fail to penetrate and soften my heart.

Listen to the next paragraph of Lincoln's proclamation:

"In the midst of a civil war of unequalled magnitude and severity ..."

Did you just hear that part? In the midst of a civil war of unequalled magnitude and severity ... this was 1863, right in the middle in the civil war! Lincoln made Thanksgiving a holiday right in the middle of the civil war!

"...which has sometimes seemed to foreign States to invite and to provoke their aggression, peace has been preserved with all nations, order has been maintained, the laws have been respected and obeyed, and harmony has prevailed everywhere except in the theatre of military conflict; while that theatre has been greatly contracted by the advancing armies and navies of the Union."

Peace has been preserved, order maintained, harmony has prevailed everywhere. Huh? Was Lincoln nuts? Or was he on to something that I need to remember: Thanksgiving is not determined by our current circumstances. I don't need to feel thankful to be thankful. This was in the middle of the civil war for goodness sake!

In Paul's first letter to the Thessalonians something similar was happening. He had been kicked out of Philippi,and it is thought that he wrote this letter from Corinth.

But look what he says, 'we give thanks to God always for you all..'

God, don't forget about God in all of this- Lincoln didn't. His next paragraph reads: "No human counsel hath devised nor hath any mortal hand worked out these great things. They are the gracious gifts of the Most High God, who, while dealing with us in anger for our sins, hath nevertheless remembered mercy."

Gracious gifts from God, right in the middle of a civil war. We thank God for you Thessalonians- your work of faith, labor of love, patience of hope in Jesus! That's what I want! No matter what happens, no matter what happens around me I want the Thessalonians work of faith, labor of love and patience of hope in Jesus. I know that Jesus wins in the end, we just read the end last chapter or so. I want patience of hope for that win!

Back to I Thessalonians 1,verse 5: 'you didn't just hear the word, but the power of the Holy Spirit in much assurance.' That translation isn't powerful enough, much assurance makes it sound like there could be more assurance; no! Full assurance, most certain confidence, there is no doubt about it would be a better understanding.

And now verse 6: 'You became followers in affliction, but with the joy of the Holy Spirit.' I want that same joy of the Holy Spirit- it's still here, it hasn't changed, why do we tend to forget as Lincoln said?

Look what all that means in verses 7-8: 'You became examples to all the other believers, the word of the Lord sounded forth in every place!'

Your faith in God is so famous that we do not need to even say anything. That's powerful, that's how we want to be- famous in our faith, no words necessary.

And verses 9-10: your faith is so famous that people notice how you turned to God from idols and how you patiently wait for Christ's return. Even Jesus who delivers us from wrath to come.

We are free from God's judgment, what could we be more thankful for than that?

Thanksgiving- whether we feel like it or not we will celebrate it as a country the last Thursday in November. Even in the midst of war, we are thankful for God's blessings and mercies. And with that thanksgiving comes the patience to wait for the glorious return of Jesus; maybe today!

# DEAR SMYRNA, HANG IN THERE

*The Revelation 2:8-11*

Did you remember to be thankful this week even if you didn't feel like it? I sure didn't feel like it as I was struggling with some crazy infection. I went to our family doctor on Monday, he looked at and said oh wow, that looks bad! He told me to call the dentist right away as he thought there was something going on with a tooth.

Tuesday I made it to the dentist, he looked at it and said, oh wow, that looks bad. It must be, you're the second doctor in two days to tell me that. Now can you fix it?

After x-rays and messing around in my mouth he said that tooth has to come out, now. Now? Right now? Thanksgiving is coming up, what about turkey and stuffing and cranberry stuff?

The dental assistant said don't worry, this is a routine procedure. Routine for whom? I've never had a tooth removed before. I like my teeth in my mouth thank you. Well, tooth number fourteen is out of my mouth and in the trash and the antibiotic is clearing up the infection. By next Thanksgiving I'll be able to eat turkey again. Funny I haven't lost any weight.

No it's easy to sit back and laugh after the ordeal is over but sometimes when we're in the middle of it, it just feels hopeless. I know we live in a war zone, I know the war is spiritual, but sometimes I just want to surrender-that's enough already, I give up! It doesn't work that way does it?

Besides knowing that Jesus (and we) wins in the end, there is something built into us by God that just knows to keep going. Hope deferred makes the heart grow sick it says in Proverbs. God has given us the ability to hope.

I read a book this week by Captain Gerald Coffee, he was a POW in Vietnam for seven years. Seven years. For seven years he kept his faith in God and he never lost hope.

All of this made me think back to the Epistles of Jesus that we started in The Revelation. A few chapters ago we saw what Jesus said to the church at Ephesus and the warning that He gave them. We looked at the pattern that each letter basically follows: Jesus identifies Himself, commends the church (if there is something to commend), points out any offense or accusation, then gives them a warning and a promise.

Well the next church in Chapter 2 of The Revelation is special in a certain way, Smyrna. Some of the symbolism found in the church in Smyrna: this is where myrrh comes from. Remember the 'wise men' visiting the baby Jesus with gold, frankincense and myrrh? An interesting thing about myrrh: it only gives off it's sweet, spicy aroma once the leaves are crushed.

Surely our griefs He Himself bore,
And our sorrows He carried;
Yet we ourselves esteemed Him stricken,
Smitten of God, and afflicted.
But He was pierced through for our transgressions,
He was crushed for our iniquities;
The chastening for our well-being *fell* upon Him,
And by His scourging we are healed. Isaiah 53:4-5

Here is the real Christmas Story from Isaiah. I know that we like the cute little Baby Jesus in the manger and Linus reading Luke chapter 2 in the Charlie Brown Christmas special. But that's not the story: the cute, chubby little baby Jesus was born into a world at war! Goodness, Herod tried to kill Him by murdering every baby in Bethlehem! And the Romans eventually did kill him. But that's not the end of the story either.

Revelation chapter 2 verse 8: Jesus is the First and the Last, who was dead, not just mostly dead but completely dead, and came to life again! Never to die again!

Look at verse 9: I know, says Jesus. Does that give us hope? Great hope because Jesus knows. I know your works, your trials and your poverty. But you are rich in Heaven! I know the blasphemy of those who claim to be Jews but are really worshipping in a synagogue of Satan.

This church was under attack from Roman Imperialists who worshipped Caesar as a god and from Jews trying to stamp out these annoying Christians who claim that Jesus is Messiah. Smyrna is where Polycarp, the church leader in about 155 AD will be burned at the stake by Romans and Jews alike for refusing to sacrifice to Caesar. History says that the Jews even carried the wood for Polycarp's execution even though it was on the Sabbath!

I know what you're going through says Jesus because I've been there. And did you notice that though we have the pattern that these letters follow, there is no accusation against the church in Smyrna. None.

Even while living in the midst of the synagogues of Satan, living with the worship of the Roman Emperor and any other god the Romans can think of, or anything else that they make into a god. In the midst of all this evil and tribulation and poverty, Jesus has nothing to say against them. Pretty impressive huh? Maybe.

Maybe that's what the church needs to be focused on? The right things like Jesus. Maybe poverty and persecution bring about doctrinal purity? Maybe riches and health and safety make us apathetic, uncaring, a little lazy in our doctrine?

Later on in Revelation 3:17, the church at Laodicea says that they are rich, they have need of nothing. But Jesus says that they are poor, blind, and naked. This rich and wealthy church is the one he vomits out of His mouth; the church in poverty and persecution he has no accusation against at all. I don't like discomfort but I know this, I'd rather be the church in Smyrna than Laodicea.

It sure appears that it is better to be poor and persecuted than rich and in need of nothing.

My brethren, count it all joy when you fall into various trials, knowing that the testing of your faith produces patience, says James 1:2-3

And not only *that*, but we also glory in tribulations, knowing that tribulation produces perseverance; and perseverance, character; and character, hope, reads Romans 5:3-5.

Do these verses make better sense now? Count it all joy in various trials? Glory in tribulations? Do you see it clearly? And listen to verse 5 of Romans 5: Now hope does not disappoint, because the love of God has been poured out in our hearts by the Holy Spirit who was given to us.

Of course! When I think of myself of being rich, wealthy and in need of nothing, I am only fooling myself. When I am in poverty and tribulations and thrust into persecution from the synagogues of Satan- that's where I build faith, patience, perseverance, character, and finally ... hope.

Here is something for us to think about as I do not have an answer but I wonder: why, oh why do we spend so much energy trying to relieve ourselves of trials and tribulations? I'm not suggesting that we should not go to the doctor or dentist and have the offending tooth removed.

But why, oh why do we wring our hands and act like something is wrong, that we have done something wrong when trials and tribulations come? Thank God, my faith is growing and building up my hope! Can I be thankful even if I don't feel that way?

Back to Revelation 2, verse 10. Here is good news: you are about to suffer, it's only going to get worse. We are not sure what the ten days refers to here, historians say that there were ten specific attempts by Rome to eradicate Christianity; Emperor Diocletian just happened to be the tenth emperor of Rome and he spent his ten years in power persecuting Christians severely.

Maybe, maybe not. One thing is for certain: be faithful until death. Huh? Man it really is going to get worse- be faithful unto death? Yes, and I will give you the crown of life says Jesus.

Short Greek lesson- the word for crown here is *stephanos*, sometimes called the crown of victory. It was the wreath of leaves that was given to the winner of the Olympic games and other organized contests. Be faithful unto death and Jesus will give us the *stephanos*. Interesting, who was the first Christian martyr? His name was Stephanos, Stephen, faithful unto death.

And verse 11: got ears? Listen up! The Spirit is telling you that he who overcomes, he who is faithful unto death will not be hurt by the second death. I thought it was appointed unto man once to die and then judgement- what's the second death?

Revelation 20:14-15, Then Death and Hades were cast into the lake of fire. This is the second death. And anyone not found written in the Book of Life was cast into the lake of fire.

The saddest words ever written. No wonder God has to wipe the tears from our eyes in Heaven. The first death is physical and temporary, the second death is spiritual and eternal. Aren't you glad for Salvation in Jesus? He was dead and now is alive so that we can be too for all of eternity.

That gives me great hope. And certainly makes me thankful, no matter what happens here on earth.

# PEACE, PEACE, BUT THERE IS NO PEACE

*Jeremiah 8:8-12*

Have you been in the Christmas Spirit this week? One of my friends was talking about the Christmas Spirit the other night and I got to thinking about it: just what is the Christmas Spirit?

I understand playing Christmas music, putting up Christmas lights and decorations, going on the hay wagon ride at Country Christmas, all those things are designed to get us in the Christmas Spirit.

I've been playing Christmas music since right before Thanksgiving, does that put me in the Christmas Spirit? Maybe the kind of music helps? The last week I've played Handel's Messiah over and over again- I just love it this time of year. Is that the Christmas Spirit? The Hallelujah Chorus?

Maybe it's shopping? What news I've read says that retail sales are doing very, very well this year. And the stock market has hit record highs. Maybe because a new president got elected and everybody is at peace about the economy and the future of our country. Hmmm, I really need to think about that one.

Whatever the case, I think that this elusive Christmas Spirit that I hear so much about is a feeling, maybe a feeling of good tidings of great joy which shall be all to all people ... glory to God in the highest and on earth peace, goodwill toward men? The world just goes right through those verses and ignores some of the words: unto you is born this day in the city of David, a Savior who is Christ the Lord.

The world loves peace on earth part, the goodwill toward men, my goodness we even got Aunt Agnus a Christmas present doesn't that show how much I care? Nothing says 'thinking of you' like a bottle of French perfume, Fragrance du Bovine from the dollar store. That's the Christmas Spirit!

Seriously speaking, I think this Christmas Spirit emotion that all the world is searching for is peace. I heard a pastor this week give his presentation of the Gospel through the Christmas Story and he wanted to make sure we all knew that Jesus was the Light of the World and by somehow accepting this light we have peace.

(Counselors are standing by to pray with you if you would like light and peace right now. Nah, I just want a hot chocolate and one of those Christmas cookies.)

I think that pastor forgot about the light shines in the darkness and the darkness did not comprehend it. The light shows the darkness of our hearts and our need for Jesus! What about the Lamb of God taking away the sins of the world? He never mentions sin or Salvation.

*"For a child has been born for us, a son given to us; authority rests upon his shoulders; and he is named Wonderful Counselor, Mighty God, Everlasting Father, Prince of Peace."* Isaiah 9:6-7

And from the Gospel of John:
*"Peace I leave with you; my peace I give to you. I do not give to you as the world gives. Do not let your hearts be troubled, and do not let them be afraid."* John 14:27

Oh I know for sure that the Christmas Spirit of peace is real, the Prince of Peace is real but that verse in John: my peace I give you not as the world gives. Not as the world gives.

Not as the world gives: the lights, the music even the manger scene ... those are as the world gives, that isn't lasting peace. It might give the world a warm feeling for a minute as Aunt Agnus oohs and aahs over how thoughtful we are but warm and fuzzy feelings of peace don't last.

That's what we call post-Holiday depression. Searching for what the world searches for is empty, it doesn't last. We go right back on Prozac on December 26th. (I always beat the rush and suffer my post-Holiday depression before Christmas.) And it just dawned on me while I was writing this, am I searching for something elusive, something worldly? Is that why I feel or don't feel as the case be, this Christmas Spirit?

What we read in Jeremiah was a warning to the nation of Judah and yet it was so unbelievable as these were times of peace and prosperity in the nation. So unbelievable that Jeremiah was terribly persecuted even by some of the godly kings of Judah. Like the church at Laodicea in Revelation 3 they thought that they were rich, they have become wealthy and need nothing but they do not know they are wretched, miserable, poor, blind and naked.

Look back at Jeremiah 8, verse 8-9. How can you say? God asks. The wise men are ashamed because the nation as whole has rejected the word of the Lord.

Verse 10: from the least to the greatest everyone is given to covetousness, even though their black Friday sales set retail records, the prophets and the priests deal falsely.

Verse 11: any wounds that God's people have suffered they literally have taken as superficial. Anyone loyal to the Lord was persecuted and then blown off- 'I was only kidding. You're not really hurt.'

Peace, peace, but there is no peace.

And now verse 12: aren't you even ashamed? He asks. No, they didn't even blush.

I know that these words and warnings were written for Judah but I can't help but think how much it sounds like our country today. False scribes, everyone so materialistic, even the priests deal falsely, taking persecution like abortion so lightly. Are we not ashamed, are we not embarrassed? Can't we learn from their mistakes? What in the world do we think is going to happen?

Well, the good news is this, there is a peace in Jesus, an eternal peace, not like the world's peace but a real peace.

Therefore, having been justified by faith, we have peace with God through our Lord Jesus Christ, through whom also we have access by faith into this grace in which we stand, and rejoice in hope of the glory of God. Romans 5:1-2

There's the part the world misses. There is what the world's Christmas Spirit can't touch. There is what doesn't get mentioned much anymore among the decorations and the music and the hot chocolate and cookies and presents.

Let's be different than the world, let's know the real peace of Jesus, the real Christmas Spirit that only comes with repentance of sin and salvation in Christ.

Because you know what? That Christmas Spirit isn't just for Christmas, it's for all year long.

Go in peace.

# EXCEEDING JOY

*Jude 20-25*

I have to admit that sometimes I really do not like the pomp and circumstance that sometimes surrounds the church setting, I am more informal. But there certainly are times when we lose something by being informal- informality can degrade into irreverence at times, and I do not want to be irreverent to God or traditions or even formalities.

I like lighting the Advent candles, I enjoy what we call the Advent season. Advent simply means a time of waiting, specifically a time of waiting for Christmas in these modern times. Why we only choose to wait for four weeks I do not know. Maybe you have heard me say before that I like the waiting more than I like the event sometimes.

I came across this famous quote: "After a time, you may find that having is not so pleasing a thing as wanting ..." Any Star Trek fans will be pleased to know that was Mr. Spock.

Anticipation may be more exciting than getting. I do not think that is true as we look at the original Advent, the waiting for Messiah, and waiting, and waiting, and waiting, for thousands of years. And finally, Jesus is born! Joy to the world, the Lord is finally come, let earth receive her King. But of course we know that earth doesn't receive her King. He came unto His own and His own received Him not ...

Anticipation may be more exciting than getting. I know that is true as we wait for the return of Messiah. There are times where the waiting isn't all that much fun at all. And yet we know that ... the sufferings of this present time are not worthy *to be compared* with the glory which shall be revealed in us.

Heaven is going to be awesome, more than I can even imagine: But as it is written, Eye hath not seen, nor ear heard, neither have entered into the heart of man, the things which God hath prepared for them that love him.

"I can only imagine," sings the group Mercy Me, and it makes for a nice song but no, no we cannot even imagine. This is a case where Mercy Me and Spock are both wrong: we can't imagine the glory that will be revealed IN US, and having is more to be unbelievably more pleasing than wanting. (And I love that song! And I love the anticipation of Advent.)

Here we are in the 2017th year of the Return of Christ Advent season, give or take a few years. Why do I enjoy the anticipation of the Christmas Advent more than the anticipation of the Rapture Advent? Maybe I need to re-think my attitude?

Which brings me back to the Epistle of Jude. I have always thought that this was a strange little letter, it takes longer to translate and explain it than it does to read through it. I really think that shows how deep it is, Jude really challenges the reader.

Now when we write letters we start out with the name of the person we are writing to: dear grandma, then what we want to say, thank you for the cookies, and then the close, love, Billy (you get the point).

Most often letters in the culture of New Testament times were different: they start out with the name of the person writing the letter, not who it is addressed to. Verse 1 tells us it is Jude, and now we see his qualifications to write: a bondservant of Jesus Christ and the brother of James. Interesting, there really is only one James who Jude could be referring to here: James, the brother of Jesus. He wrote a letter a little earlier remember?

Matthew 13:55, 'Is not this the carpenter's son? is not his mother called Mary? and his brethren, James, and Joses, and Simon, and Judas?' Yes, this is the carpenter's son but not the Son of the carpenter, He is the very Son of God. But this is His earthly family: James, Joses, Simon and His youngest brother Judas, or Jude.

We know that Jesus's family thought that He was crazy, but tradition says that as the Risen Lord He appeared especially to James, and thus James and obviously Jude became born again believers. Can you imagine how cool that would be?

Back to verse 1, Jude, qualifications, and now: to those who are called, sanctified and preserved ... We are not sure who exactly received this letter or what time it was written, but that really doesn't matter; it was written to us!

Jude's letter calls the church to be aware, be careful of apostasy, false teachers, creeping in and doing great damage in the early church. He starts with some history of evil infiltrating God's people and warns us that it is still happening today. You can read the letter for yourself and ask me if there is something hard to understand ... I may not know the answer, we'll have to figure it out together.

But it was those last few verses that really seemed to get my attention this week, verses 20-21. Keep going, keep building yourself up in faith, holy faith, keep praying, keep yourself in the love of God, looking for the mercy of our Lord Jesus Christ to eternal life.

I have to tell you that the Greek word translated 'looking' isn't strong enough. It can literally mean 'to expect the fulfillment of promises'. "... keep your selves in the love of God, expecting the fulfillment of the promise of mercy of our Lord Jesus Christ unto eternal life." Expect it, Jesus promised it!

Verses 22-23: while you're waiting have compassion, and some people will need to be pulled out of the fire, but remember this is a letter about apostasy and false teachers, hating even their defiled clothes. Jude pulls no punches, like his brother James he does not know political correctness. Thank God!

And now we come to the end of the letter, where we would write love, Sammy. Look what Jude says in verse 24: now to Him, who can keep you from stumbling and present you faultless before the presence of His glory, with exceeding joy!

Oh I love that word: exceeding joy, indescribable joy, unimaginable joy. No, we can't even imagine. Sorry Mercy Me but this word has nothing comparable in English, it is a joy beyond description, exceeding joy? You better believe it! And even more than that! Eye has not seen, ear has not heard ... this is joy beyond joy.

And now verse 25: ' ... to the only God our Savior be glory, majesty, power and authority, through Jesus Christ our Lord, before all ages, now and forevermore! Amen.'

That is an interesting way to end a letter. Maybe we could use that as an example? Both now and forever. We seem to easily forget that now part don't we? Now and forever, God is now and forever, oh help us remember that as we wait for Messiah to return.

Hang in there says Jude. Be faithful, keep praying, stay in the love of God, watch for the return of Christ unto eternal life. Let's remember the exceeding joy waiting for us.

Exceeding joy. May God fill your heart with such joy, both now, and forever. As we wait for Rapture. Amen.

# CRAZY LOVE

I *John* 4:7-11

The fourth Sunday of Advent is commonly called the Sunday of love. Listen to the words from the Advent reading:

"Jesus demonstrated self-giving love in his ministry as the Good Shepherd. Advent is a time for kindness, thinking of others, and sharing with others. It is a time to love as God loved us by giving us his most precious gift. As God is love, let us be love also."

Well that all sounds nice but when I really think about it what does Jesus as the Good Shepherd have to do with love? I think we see Jesus's love better in the verses we read in I John 4, especially verse 10: 'In this is love, not that we loved God, but that He loved us and sent His Son *to be* the propitiation for our sins.'

And the next sentence says that Advent is a time for kindness ... the other 48 weeks of the year I don't have to worry about kind to other people. Funny thing- as I was thinking about all of this the mail came at the office.

The mailman delivered a package to the door, two packages actually, and I heard my wife Teresa say 'is there any other mail?' Oh yeah sure, but you have to go out to the box and get it. That's not the first time- I watched the mailman stop at the box at the end of the driveway one day after dropping a package off at the house.

I was having a really hard time feeling loving right then. But why? Listen to these verses from Deuteronomy 10 that are sometimes read for Advent: 'For the Lord your God *is* God of gods and Lord of lords, the great God, mighty and awesome, who shows no partiality nor takes a bribe. He administers justice for the fatherless and the widow, and loves the stranger, giving him food and clothing.'

And in Matthew chapter 5 Jesus makes it all very, very clear: "You have heard that it was said, 'You shall love your neighbor and hate your enemy.' But I say to you, love your enemies, bless those who curse you, do good to those who hate you, and pray for those who spitefully use you and persecute you, that you may be sons of your Father in heaven; for He makes His sun rise on the evil and on the good, and sends rain on the just and on the unjust."

Love your enemies, bless those who make you walk out to the mailbox in freezing weather even though they just drove up to the door to deliver a package. (Actually, Teresa went out in the cold, and snow, not me.)

I began to think this: why do I base my love for people on what they do or don't do? God doesn't. Love based on performance or the lack of performance is not love. Read that again: Love based on performance or the lack of performance is not love.

Look at I John again and back up just a few verses in I John 3:11-12: 'For this is the message that ye heard from the beginning, that we should love one another. Not as Cain, who was of that wicked one, and slew his brother. And wherefore slew he him? Because his own works were evil, and his brother's righteous.'

Cain hated Able because of his works, because of his performance, his righteous performance in this particular case. And while Cain paid a terrible price being alienated from his family for the rest of his life, the sun still shined on him and the rain still fell upon him. God still blessed him whether he recognized it or not, it wasn't based on his performance, good or evil.

I really need to think about this one- God's love is not based upon performance? What about being born-again, getting saved? Doesn't God love His children and hate the evil ones? Jacob I loved, but Esau I hated, what about that verse? Of course, the sun still shined and the rain still fell on Esau ...

Love your enemies "...that you may be sons of your Father in heaven; for He makes His sun rise on the evil and on the good, and sends rain on the just and on the unjust."

And back to I John 3 we see that "Whoever hates his brother is a murderer, and you know that no murderer has eternal life abiding in him."

I promised myself that I would not get into any Greek in this lesson. I know it doesn't necessarily help to know the Greek words, it's still God's Word. But I had to look up this sentence to see if it was maybe saying something else or something more: 'whoever hates his brother is a murderer.'

So in Greek it actually says that 'whoever hates his brother is a murderer.' And the word translated brother, could be family, could be countrymen, could be anyone of the human race, it's pretty broad. So, whoever hates his brother is a murderer. There is now way around it, the meaning is clear. (I'm beginning to like that mailman better already..)

Last week I finished a book by Francis Chan called *Crazy Love*. He is a church planter in San Francisco and writes books and most of his sermons you can get on YouTube, on the internet. No church building anymore, just log on.

This book, *Crazy Love* sold over 2 million copies.

Funny, it got great reviews, sold millions of copies, and yet I was a little disappointed with it. I was hoping to read something about God's crazy love for me. You know, the 'while we were yet sinners Christ died for us' kind of love.

I wanted to read how ridiculous and crazy that God's love is for me, because you know what? Sometimes not only do I not feel like loving, but I don't feel loved, or even lovable. Well I didn't find what I was looking for in Francis Chan's book although 2 million other people apparently did.

Why do I look in the wrong places anyway? Here is the only place I'm going to find what I'm looking for, what I need. That's the Bible.

Remember a while back that I quoted Dave Fullen's song *The Poser*?

Listen to the words to the final chorus:

I turn toward home
I have a moment of clarity
What I truly want, what I truly need
What I really want, the me I need to be
What I truly want, what I truly need
comes from Jesus.

In a moment of clarity I realize that what I really want, what I truly need comes from Jesus. Nowhere else, no one else!

So, if you still have your finger at I John 4:7-11, maybe we can bring this all together to make sense:

Look at verses 7-9: Beloved, let us love one another, for love is of God; and everyone who loves is born of God and knows God. He who does not love does not know God, for God is love. In this the love of God was manifested toward us, that God has sent His only begotten Son into the world, that we might live through Him.

And then verse 10 sums it up: 'not that we loved God, but that He loved us', me ... so much that Jesus became the propitiation, that is the appeasing for my sin. That's what I needed to hear. That's the real crazy love, the ridiculous love of God.

And finally verse 11: if God loved, so we also ought to love one another, the mailman, and anybody else that it might be really, really hard to love sometimes.

In this is love, not that we loved God, but that He loved us and sent His Son *to be* the propitiation for our sins. Beloved, if God so loved us, we also ought to love one another.

Let's be those kind of people, this time of year and any time of year.

# BRAND NEW

*Jesus Promises*
*Matthew 19:23-30*

I am writing this just before the start of a new year. Did you ever think that we would be around this long? I think many people really thought that Jesus would have returned by now but of course, folks have been thinking that for about 2,017 plus years now. We'll just have to keep waiting ...

Of course waiting isn't so bad, remember what Paul said to the Romans? "And yet we know that ... the sufferings of this present time are not worthy *to be compared* with the glory which shall be revealed in us." We know that, he said. Doesn't take much faith when we know something for sure.

And just in case you forget that we know that, Paul tells the Corinthians, "Eye hath not seen, nor ear heard, neither have entered into the heart of man, the things which God hath prepared for them that love him."

My mind cannot quite comprehend it all but the New Heaven and the new earth are going to be awesome. Brand new! Everything. Untouched by sin and corruption. No wonder this life, no matter how much suffering we deal with cannot even compare to eternity.

In the early 1980's when Teresa and I were first married and I was much younger and tougher, I worked for Piqua Granite and Marble. My job was to drive the truck and do the monument construction. That's a fancy term for putting up tombstones. Teresa and I like to walk through old cemeteries and once in a while where I can still find some of my work. It is very peaceful there.

It all makes for really interesting stories but what I was thinking about this week is a fellow I used to work with, Russ. Russ was a skinny old hillbilly, smoked like a freight train, and could fix just about anything. He was the stereotypical shade tree mechanic. My guess is that he worked at Piqua Granite for benefits, probably health insurance.

Russ was such a likeable guy, I really enjoyed working with him because he had an interesting way of looking at things, at life, and he had funny little sayings for just about anything that happened. "Don't get excited," was his trade mark saying. We got an 80 ton construction crane stuck in the yard at the Shelby County courthouse. Don't get excited, said Russ. Oh I'm not excited, I figure we can get it out by next June when the yard dries out.

50 tons of fully polished granite could be swinging wildly out of control 30 feet in the air and Russ, well he just didn't get excited. He was right, it always worked out, here I am safe and sound. I have all of my fingers and toes and if you don't count the one back surgery I needed, then we scored a perfect safety record.

My favorite saying that Russ was always using ... once something was fixed or repaired, or returned to its nearly original state, Russ would be proud of the work and he would congratulate himself and everyone else by saying, "Brand new." You have to say it with a southern drawl, "Brand new," stressing the last syllable and sometimes adding what you were fixing: "Brand new monument, brand new truck, brand new whatever." I sure miss Russ. I heard that he passed away some time ago. Those were great times in life and I didn't know it.

Brand new. Russ would think it's really funny to be quoting him in a book some 35 years later.

As we look back at Matthew 19:23-30, we see that there is a lot going on here. Jesus is straightening out some bad theology that riches and blessings are the sign of God's favor; you must be a great guy, you're rich!

Now you can read this again for yourself but I want to focus on one verse, no, one word really. Now how in the world can you make a lesson out of just one word? We'll try it ...

Let's set it up starting at verse 27: Then Peter answered and said to Him, "See, we have left all and followed You. Therefore what shall we have?"

That is just like Peter at this point in his life, always looking out for number one. And in reality, it is a legitimate question: we have given up everything for you Jesus, what do we get out of it? I think that Peter is accustomed to Jesus's rebuke. Goodness, Jesus calls him Satan on at least one occasion.

Do you think that every pastor, missionary, and person totally sold out for Jesus doesn't think this once in a while? It would be so phony of me to say that I'm not looking forward to that crown of life, the new, no make that 'brand new' white stone, the morning star, and all the other benefits Jesus promises 'to him who overcomes'.

Of course we think that way on occasion. I have left all that the world has to offer to follow you Jesus. What shall I have?

Jesus just answers the question, without rebuke, it is a legitimate question: So Jesus said to them, "Assuredly I say to you, that in the regeneration, when the Son of Man sits on the throne of His glory, you who have followed Me will also sit on twelve thrones, judging the twelve tribes of Israel.

Sounds good to me. But the word that really has my attention is this: regeneration. In the regeneration when Jesus takes His throne ... in the regeneration. I think that everyone listening knew exactly what Jesus meant using that word, regeneration, and the way He used it. "In the regeneration" in Greek, you know I have to throw in some Greek somewhere, is *pal-ing-ghen-es-ee'-ah*. It is a compound word: *palin*, meaning anew, again, and *genesis*, meaning birth, first time. Does that sound familiar?

The regeneration. It's Genesis all over again, a new earth, brand new. Imagine for a minute that everything we know is made brand new, untainted by sin and corruption. We can't, can we? We have never known a brand new world, but we will! Will it have that new earth smell like a new car? Brand new- that sure is something to look forward to. Brand new!

Like the new year. A brand new year. This our opportunity to be brand new people. Every morning with the Lord is a do-over, his mercies are new every morning and a brand new year is a major do over.

What about new year resolutions? Have you ever kept any? That's too shallow, I need a *palinggenesia* in my heart and my attitude and that only comes from salvation in Christ. What an incredible way to begin a new year. And every one that hath forsaken houses, or brethren, or sisters, or father, or mother, or wife, or children, or lands, for my name's sake, shall receive an hundredfold, and shall inherit everlasting life.

Have you given up on this old world and found salvation in Jesus? Make today the day. What's in it for me you ask like Peter? Well, only eternal life. Please don't close this book without the assurance of Jesus.

Listen to these words from Isaiah, a glimpse of what lies ahead in the regeneration:
"Do not remember the former things,
Nor consider the things of old.
Behold, I will do a new thing,
Now it shall spring forth;
Shall you not know it?
I will even make a road in the wilderness
And rivers in the desert.
The beast of the field will honor Me,
The jackals and the ostriches,

Because I give waters in the wilderness
*And* rivers in the desert,
To give drink to My people, My chosen.
This people I have formed for Myself;
They shall declare My praise.

I didn't mention it before, but I wasn't born again until 1994, many years after working with Russ.

Boy, I sure hope that Russ found Jesus like I did and that he is there in eternity, brand new.

# THOUGH, THOUGH, THOUGH, YET ...

*Habakkuk 3:17-19*

It's funny how things go sometimes in life, little twists and turns that you really don't expect and don't seem to mean much when they happen. We look back and say, huh, that was interesting, I wonder what all of that meant.

Now you need to know that I do believe what Paul wrote in the book of Romans that all things work together for good to those who love God. But not everything means something. For example, do you know Christians who say things like, oh, I wish I could know what God has for me to learn so I can get over this cold?

Maybe you just got a cold. Ever think of that? Do you really think that God has smitten you with a cold to learn something or as some form of discipline? Maybe you just got a cold.

Hey, what if it was God but you didn't learn the lesson? Do you get another cold right away? Or how about the flu? Maybe next time God will send you the flu to get your attention? See how silly that all sounds?

Maybe I say all of that because I had a cold last weekend; didn't seem to learn a thing. Uh-oh, hope you had your flu shot!

Well, some funny things happened last week that did not seem to mean a thing and yet some twists and turns did make me think. I didn't learn anything but it did make me think.

My son asked me to edit a few chapters of a book that he is writing; what little I read of it sure seems like a great work to me. But in the chapters I read I noticed an awkward sentence construction that he seemed to overuse, a lot. He writes like he talks and he annoyingly uses the word 'though', a lot.

Examples- "Before we really approach these questions <u>though</u>, let's talk about what it means to know something."

The very next paragraph: "With any knowledge <u>though</u>, there is a measure of doubt, and usually that doubt centers on the second part of knowing, the truth part."

First paragraph, next chapter: "If you watch <u>though</u>, you will notice ..."you get the idea, too many <u>thoughs</u>! I reminded him of that old English proverb, when in doubt, leave it out. I think that his final draft will have less.

Then something later in the week sent me to the book of Habakkuk. Habakkuk is asking why God, why do the wicked prosper? When oh, when will they finally get justice? Like a really, really bad cold?

God answers and tells Habakkuk that judgment is coming, worse than a bad cold, but it's in God's time, not Habakkuk's.

Something funny I noticed about the last few verses of Habakkuk: Though the fig tree may not blossom, nor fruit be on the vines; though the labor of the olive may fail, and the fields yield no food; though the flock may be cut off from the fold, and there be no herd in the stalls-

Good thing Habakkuk didn't ask me to edit his book, eh? I would have thrown out all of the <u>thoughs</u>, they seem so redundant.

Now another funny thing: maybe your Bible does not translate the same way New King James does and you do not have all those <u>thoughs</u>. See, I wouldn't be so out of line to remove them now would I?

The word 'though' and 'although' are difficult enough in English. Used as conjunctions the two are interchangeable. But 'though' can be used as an adverb and then they are not interchangeable. And, neither word actually appears in the Hebrew.

Whew! That's enough grammar lesson for today. The point is that if my son hadn't been so excited using the word in his writing I would have never noticed anything in the last few verses of Habakkuk. I probably would have passed right over it.

So look again at verse 17: Though the fig tree may not blossom, nor fruit be on the vines; though the labor of the olive may fail, and the fields yield no food; though the flock may be cut off from the fold, and there be no herd in the stalls-

These sound like pretty terrible times. The figs are gone, the grapes are gone, all the work we put into the olive groves failed, and the crops failed. On top of that the flocks are cut off somewhere and there are no herds in the stalls. We're going to starve!

Verse 18: Yet I will rejoice in the Lord, I will joy in the God of my salvation. If the word <u>though</u> wasn't difficult enough now we have the word <u>yet</u>. There is a Hebrew word for yet, meaning again, repeatedly, again and again, but this is not it! The sentence literally reads: And I in Yahweh I-shall-be-joyous, I-shall-exult in Elohim-of salvation-of me:

Are you thankful for English translations?

Let's tie all of these thoughts together: even though our agricultural society has completely failed as the result of God's judgement (this is easy to see, it is not just a cold) I will rejoice in the Lord, I will joy in the God of my salvation.

I tell you what, Habakkuk has more faith than I have. He has joy, he will rejoice, he will exult in God anyway despite dire circumstances?

Is there something wrong with me? Why don't I wake with a joyful heart? Joy was just here. Where did it go?

In a recent devotion, Staci Eldredge wrote this: "Now, to be fair, joy isn't exactly falling from the sky these days. We don't go out to gather it each morning like manna. It's hard to come by. Joy seems more elusive than winning the lottery. We don't like to think about it much, because it hurts to allow ourselves to feel how much we long for joy, and how seldom it drops by."

She's right. It hurts to allow ourselves to feel how much we long for joy, and it hurts when we think of how easy our joy is stolen with something so simple as a mean word. How often do you hear people say that Satan wants to steal our joy? He does a really good job of it by using people to say and do evil things.

Staci Eldredge went on: "But joy *is* the point. I know it is. God says that joy is our strength. "The joy of the Lord is your strength" (Nehemiah 8:10). I think, *My strength? I don't even think of it as my occasional boost.* But yes, now that I give it some thought, I can see that when I have felt joy I have felt more alive than at any other time in my life."

Great Staci, I fully agree but how in the world do my emotions match Habakkuk's and I joy in the Lord in spite of my circumstance? How do I keep the mean and evil things said about me from stealing my joy? I know there is more to circumstance than what we are living in this world, I know that the evil said is not true- but how do I stay focused on God like Habakkuk?

I'll tell you plainly- I don't know. It's a process, it's a destination where I have not arrived.

There is a hint of how-to in verse 19: The Lord God is my strength; He will make my feet like deer's *feet*, And He will make me walk on my high hills.

There are some things in this verse that we need to notice: Habakkuk uses a compound name for God, Yahweh Adonai, Lord and Master.

The words translated 'my strength' could be said to mean my ability.

And notice that the Lord and Master will make my feet walk on high places, according to my ability to obey the Lord and Master.

Books have been written and sermons preached about these high places and usually we are given the vision of some mountainous experience. He will make me walk on my high hills.

Here is a better vision of what Habakkuk means: As a teenager I spent a lot of time in the wilds of northern Michigan and if you've been there often you know that much of the inland state is covered by swamps. There is only one way to get through a swamp. You have to step on the high places, the tufts of grass and weeds that grow up high out of the swamp.

Miss one of the high places and guess what? Into the muck and mire you go. The deer can do it, the moose don't care.

Here is the key to faithful joy, let God be your strength to make you tread on the high places, to stay out of the mire and muck of evil tongued people and the swamp of this world's culture. Let God place your steps on those high places.

You have nothing to lose, and only joy to gain. No matter what happens.

# NEVER GIVE UP, NEVER, NEVER, NEVER GIVE UP.

*Hebrews 10:35-38*

There was a headline in the news a few years back that got my attention. Folks who believe in end times prophecy probably noticed too. It said: *Obama Tells United Nations We Will Submit To a World Government.* Hmmm, that's a little scary. I always wonder why I am surprised when we clearly see prophecy being fulfilled?

Some of my anticipation is that I want it to happen now, I do not have much patience. Let's have the Rapture right now and get things over with. But that's not the way it works, is it?

We are charged to have patience, endurance, the faith to keep going, to overcome even when it seems like God is never going to move. He does, he is just more patient than I.

The book of Hebrews is a discourse of encouragement to keep going, do not turn back, do not give up, do not give in. Many Jewish people were beginning to go back to the Law, to give up on Christianity, just like their ancestors tried to go back to Egypt so many years before.

There is some strong language in this letter as many times God says in wrath, 'they shall not enter my rest'. He says it is impossible for those who were once enlightened to be renewed if they fall away. Those words should scare us more than the one world government being planned by the U.N.

These words of encouragement in Hebrews 10 reminded me of the famous speech given by Winston Churchill during World War II. Many of my friends have the quote in the signature of their e-mails, "Never give up. Never, never, never give up."

Have you heard the story behind that speech? Churchill was invited to the school he attended as a boy to give some words of encouragement. As the story goes, he got up speak, said, "Never give up. Never, never, never give up," and then sat back down.

It surely makes for a great story but I am going to ruin it for you; it's not true! (That makes us wonder how many other things we believe to be true are not? I have been told and re-told that story many times in my life; but it's not true!)

On October 29, 1941, Winston Churchill did indeed make a speech to the staff and students of Harrow School. He spoke for fifteen to twenty minutes, a very normal length speech, and in the middle of his closing remarks he said this, "Never give in. Never give in. Never, never, never—in nothing, great or small, large or petty—never give in, except to convictions of honour and good sense. Never yield to force. Never yield to the apparently overwhelming might of the enemy."

It still makes for a great quote even though Churchill did not say what we think he said. That sounds like a Yogi Berra quote. Now don't tell me that all the things Yogi said he really didn't say!

Never give in, never, never, never ... We see a similar pattern here in Hebrews 10:35-36: "Therefore do not cast away your confidence, which has great reward. For you have need of endurance, so that after you have done the will of God, you may receive the promise."

Don't throw away the confidence you have in Christ Jesus; in his perfect sacrifice. You can read the whole chapter of Hebrews 10 for yourself and see who and why we can such confidence in Christ.

Don't throw it away, it has great reward! Great reward he says. I know we like to think that well, I am not working for rewards, it's just because I love Jesus so much. I wouldn't want anyone to think I'm selfish or something.

Let me ask, what are you going to do when Jesus hands you the crown of glory? Refuse it? Do you know how insulting it is to refuse someone trying to give you something, let alone something that you have earned? No thanks Jesus, just keep your crown, or give it to someone who really needs it. Do you realize how foolish that sounds?

And what gift will you have to cast at his feet if you refuse yours? You will have insulted Jesus twice: first by not receiving what he has promised and second by having nothing to offer back!

Verse 36 again: you need endurance he says. Boy is that ever true, I need endurance. How many times have I just felt like giving up, going back to Egypt?

But I need endurance verse 36 says, so that after I have done the will of God I may receive the promise. Now apparently giving up is not the will of God, endurance to carry on is the will of God. And then the promise. What promise?

Verse 37: The soon return of Jesus. He who is coming will come, guaranteed, and will not tarry. It just seems like a long time to me.

And verse 38: Now the just shall live by faith. Of course, we have heard that many times, we just need the endurance to live by faith. "But if anyone draws back, My soul has no pleasure in him", says the Lord. The writer of Hebrews is quoting Habakkuk here; interesting isn't it? We just looked at Habakkuk.

And verse 39: "We are not of those who draw back to perdition," we read some very strong language again. Those who go back to perdition, which means utter ruin, complete and unfixable ruin.

Now we see why God says several times that they will not enter his rest; it is impossible to be redeemed from perdition.

"But we are of those who believe to the saving of the soul." Oh, beloved aren't you thankful for that? There is motivation enough for me to keep going, to endure, to live by faith, to not go back no matter how tempting it may appear, no matter how much easier it looks.

Never give in, never, never, never give in. Giving up, going back is a lie. I want to live by truth, by faith. I want to be counted as one of those who believe to the saving of the soul.

What else is there?

# DO NOT FEAR, BE AN ENCOURAGER

*Deuteronomy 3:23-29*

Someone shared this cute little acrostic of the word respect:
Recognize that everyone has value; Everyone has a voice; Seek to understand, then to be understood; Presume good intentions; Encourage each other; Come prepared; Timeliness is important.

The point is that respect has become hard to find in society these days. It's strange that we have no respect for authority anymore, no respect even for the winning team; we give everyone a trophy right?

And yet celebrities and professional athletes are put on a such a pedestal. We swoon over these folks as a society, and why? I've got an idea- let's give all the NFL teams a trophy for participation, even the Cleveland Browns.

Along with respect comes kindness, you can't be kind to someone you do not respect and you do not respect people that you are not kind to.

Then I came across this quote from Plato:
*"Be kind, for everyone you meet is fighting a hard battle."*

It has been said that everyone is either in the midst of the battle, just coming out of a battle, or about to enter the battle. We may not even notice as a smile or a joke often masks deep feelings and hurts.

Proverbs 14:13 says it this way, *"Even in laughter the heart may be in pain, and the end of joy may be grief."* Oh, I understand that one perfectly as that's the way I deal with hurt; I make a joke out of it.

In Deuteronomy 3 Moses pleaded with Lord to change his mind and let Moses enter the Promised Land. Didn't work did it? Moses got to see the land but not enter it.

Then God tells Moses something really interesting in verse 28, "But command Joshua, and encourage him and strengthen him; for he shall go over before this people, and he shall cause them to inherit the land which you will see."

*"Be kind, for everyone you meet is fighting a hard battle."* –Plato

It has been said that everyone is either in the midst of the battle, just coming out of a battle, or about to enter the battle. Joshua is about to enter the battle. He needs encouragement.

This "encourage" was not just a "pep talk". The meaning of the word is to *"fasten upon ... strengthen to become even stronger ... fortify"* encouragement that it would take to persevere in the days ahead.

Joshua needs a lot of encouragement as God tells him many times to, "... be strong and of good courage, do not be afraid."

He needs the 'E' in the respect acrostic, encourage each other! It is no different for us! We're either coming out of a battle, in the middle of a battle, or about to enter a battle. We need encouragement.

We love to quote that verse in Hebrews 10:25, "...not forsaking the assembling of ourselves together, as is the manner of some ..." We have all heard this admonition to remind us not to miss church. But why? Why do we assemble together?

We ignore the first part of the sentence which says, "...and let us consider how to stimulate one another to love and good deeds, not forsaking our own assembling together, as is the habit of some, but encouraging *one another*; and all the more as you see the day drawing near."

Worship is important. Sermons are wonderful. But could it be possible, that a core reason to meet together is to encourage one another? Something far beyond the "How ya doing?" and "Good to see ya!"

We need encouragement that is not just a "pep talk". The meaning of the word is to "fasten upon ... strengthen to become even stronger ... fortify;" encouragement that it would take to persevere in the days ahead. That's what we need from each other!

Now I think that there are two reasons that we need encouragement, and that we don't give encouragement.

The reason we need encouragement is fear. How many times did God tell Joshua to not be afraid? How often in Scripture do we read 'fear not'? We're afraid. That's why I make a joke out of circumstances, I am afraid.

The reason we do not give encouragement is fear. Think about that for a minute. Why am I not kind as Plato said? Why do we find it so hard to follow the rest of the verse in Hebrews 10:24-25, "...and let us consider how to stimulate one another to love and good deeds ... but encouraging *one another* ..."

Boy we are quick to tell folks that they ought to be in church, we like that part, but for some reason we are afraid "...to stimulate to love and ... encourage one another ..."

Do you know what we are afraid of? It really is simple- we are afraid of losing some kind of power and control. You can convince yourself differently. You can say, they don't deserve a kind word, they hurt me, I need to hurt them back. I am miserable with life, they need to be miserable with life.

You can tell yourself just about anything but the real reason is your fear over the loss of power and control. When you speak a kind word, when you encourage someone the point of *"fasten upon ... strengthen to become even stronger ... fortify"* like Moses did for Joshua, you are giving up a piece of self. You are acknowledging the worth of another person. You know what speaking a kind word, speaking a word of encouragement really comes down to?

Loving your neighbor as yourself.

Just like the children of Israel, we have an enemy who came to steal, kill and destroy our walk with Christ. Remember that the enemy is strong and powerful and Satan does not really need our help.

Everyone you meet is fighting a battle. Encourage them. Fortify them. Pour words of strength and courage into their hearts and spirits.

An interesting thing happens when we give up some power and control to pour ourselves into another person. We get more power and control to keep encouraging those around us. We get the same encouragement that we give.

"Stimulate to love and ... encourage one another ..." The writer of Hebrews says. Why bother trying to get people to come to church if they don't find encouragement?

Something to think about.

Love the Lord your God with all of your heart and soul and mind. Love your neighbor as yourself.

It is that simple, just not that easy.

# ABOUT THE AUTHOR

Dr. Sam Ronicker left the business world after 22 years as an executive in the newspaper industry. He and his wife Teresa, a Dayton Christian School employee for nearly 20 years, became the dorm parents at Operation Rebirth Christian Boarding Academy in March 2008.

In September 2009, Sam took over the day to day operations of the ministry and the boarding school as the Director.

Sam has a Diploma in Biblical Studies, a Bachelor of Arts degree in Christian Counseling, a Master of Divinity degree, and his Doctor of Theology degree from Atlantic Coast Theological Seminary.

Both he and Teresa are Christian Counselors and Sam serves as Pastor at Mount Pleasant Baptist Church. He has written several books and devotionals.

Sam and Teresa make their home in the city of St. Paris; have three grown children, ten grandchildren and a well behaved little dog named Charlie.

Printed in the United States
By Bookmasters